Who Is Witter Bynner?

WHO IS WITTER BYNNER?

A Biography

James Kraft

University
of
New Mexico Press
Albuquerque

Library of Congress Cataloging-in-Publication Data

Kraft, James.
Who is Witter Bynner? : a biography / James Kraft. — 1st ed.
p.   cm.
Includes bibliographical references.
ISBN 0-8263-1626-3
1. Bynner, Witter, 1881–1968—Biography.   2. Poets, American—20th
century—Biography.   I. Title.
PS3503.Y45Z75   1995
811'.52—dc20
[B]   94-18764
                                                                CIP

for
Brooks and Elizabeth
and for
Lynn and Eduardo

Contents

Acknowledgments

I wish to express my gratitude to the Witter Bynner Foundation for Poetry for its support of the research I originally completed for the five-volume edition *The Works of Witter Bynner* (1978–81). I am also grateful to the MacDowell Colony and the Millay Colony for the Arts for their fellowships to write this book. Since I completed this book, Paul Horgan has died, but my special thanks still go to him as he first introduced me to the work of Witter Bynner and encouraged me in a study of Bynner's writing and his life. I am grateful to Pat McDonald, Renée Guerrero, and Susan O'Dell, who have worked on the manuscript.

Who Is Witter Bynner?

Who is Witter Bynner? The question seems amusing, as if no one could really have been given this name. In fact, the full name was Harold Witter Bynner, and he was usually called "Hal" by his friends and signed his work Witter Bynner. At one point early in this century, it was a name as well known in poetry circles as the names of Amy Lowell, Vachel Lindsay, Carl Sandburg, and Edna St. Vincent Millay. Witter Bynner wrote for the major periodicals as well as for the little magazines, and he completed more than thirty volumes of verse and prose, mostly published by Alfred A. Knopf. He traveled twice to China, in 1917 and 1920, and translated into English two of the Chinese classics, the selection of the T'ang poets that he entitled *The Jade Mountain*, and the *Tao Teh Ching*, which Bynner called *The Way of Life according to Laotzu*. He knew D. H. and Frieda Lawrence, traveled with them on their Mexican trip in 1923, and was the original of a minor character in *The Plumed Serpent*. He wrote three poems about Lawrence and in 1951 completed a controversial account of his trip and of the Lawrences, *Journey with Genius*.

Witter Bynner was born in Brooklyn, New York, in 1881, raised in Norwich, Connecticut, and Brookline, Massachusetts, and went to Harvard with Wallace Stevens and Franklin Delano Roosevelt. Upon his graduation, he worked with Lincoln Steffens, Ida Tarbell, and Willa Cather at *McClure's* magazine, where he arranged for the first publication in this country of A. E. Housman and was one of the early champions of O. Henry. Pound's father asked Bynner if the young Ezra should be sent to Europe for the experience; Bynner readily endorsed the idea and later published Pound's first American book in 1910. Bynner wrote of his first meeting with Pound: "Although the weather was autumnal, he wore a wide-brimmed straw hat of coarse shiny weave, the band on it white with large pink polka dots. Jacket, vest, and trousers were, in my remembrance, of these colors—mauve, snuff-colored, and purplish—and his socks bright-hued in shoes one black, one blue." Bynner was a close friend of Edna St. Vincent Millay, and she accepted his proposal of marriage, a proposal they later agreed was a bad idea. In 1915 he translated Euripides' *Iphigenia in Tauris* at the request of Isadora Duncan, who wanted "a simple English text as human as the Greek, no rhymes, no inversions, no loss of meaning in sound"; in 1956 the translation was included in the University of Chicago's collected Greek plays as one of the first modern versions of Greek drama. In 1931 he edited and wrote the introduction to the sonnets of Frederick Goddard Tuckerman, including poems never before published.

For forty-seven years he lived in Santa Fe, New Mexico, thirty-four of these with one man, Robert Hunt, in a large, rambling, eccentric adobe house filled with Chinese scrolls and jade, Indian jewelry, pots, and baskets, and Hispanic *santos*. He was an early supporter of equal suffrage and an admirer and advocate of African Americans, especially their writers, of American Indians, about whom he wrote some fine poetry, and of Hispanic Americans. He also owned a house in Chapala, Mexico, and wrote well of the people of that country. An intensely devoted American, little interested in Europe and greatly committed to Walt Whitman's sense of democracy as a brotherhood, he avidly supported FDR and believed in the need for Americans to tolerate communism if the United States was to consider itself a democracy. A Rabelaisian storyteller, a sociable man who friends said could single-handedly make a party a success, a wit and punster, he and his friend Arthur Davison Ficke created the greatest hoax in American letters. For two years, in the important verse magazines, under the names of Emanuel Morgan and Anne Knish, they published the Spectra poems, a "school of poetry" created to mock the seriousness of Imagism and the pretensions of the new intellectual poetry—the poetry that later predominated in the United States and that was in part responsible for leaving Bynner an increasingly forgotten writer for the last thirty of his eighty-seven years.

Most of his life a man of means, he inherited money and became in the late 1940s a millionaire who spent like a frugal New Englander. His friend Robert Hunt, although twenty-five years younger, died in 1964. One year later, almost to the day, Bynner suffered a severe stroke that left him dependent upon nurses for his last three and a half years. During this time he existed in a silence and isolation he had intensely fought to avoid all his life.

By nature an open, generous man, and by belief one who saw no value in consistency—he frequently quoted Emerson's remark that a foolish consistency showed a little mind—he had little capacity for introspection and personal intimacy. He was too large a spirit with too quick a talent that he could too easily disperse. His own nature was impetuous and instinctual. As someone wrote to him and he then quoted to another friend: "I know of no one who enjoys life as you do and yet I feel you enjoy it to protect yourself against life."

As he grew older he did become more thoughtful, but he could not transcend this nature whose limitations he felt more and more keenly. What redeemed Bynner was the unusual degree of honesty he exhibited about his personal life. He said: "A. E. Housman wished his light verse and many variants destroyed. Willa Cather forbade printing any of her letters. I cannot imagine fear of letting people see one's frivolities and stupidities. Why always a cravat?" He let himself be seen, he left a great deal behind for us to see, and his life can be considered an exemplar of a man's struggle to engage honorably in the varied possibilities of his nature and his times and to hold on to some order, tolerance, and decency.

Who, indeed, is Witter Bynner?

≡

On a muggy day—the tenth of August 1881—Mrs. Annie Louise Bynner, née Brewer of Plainfield, Connecticut, not yet twenty-three and pregnant, accidentally dropped a bird in its cage from the second floor of a four-story brownstone in Brooklyn. In her eager attempt to reach the ground before the family cat got there, she precipitated young Harold prematurely into the world. We may delight in this symbolism: a caged bird falls to the earth and out comes a poet—but questions remain that were not directly answered. It was thought that Annie Louise was more than eight months pregnant and the incident a poetic creation to hide a serious fact.

This muggy August day was almost exactly eight months after the wedding of Annie Louise and Thomas Edgarton Bynner. About the wedding, we know that Annie wanted the word "obey" omitted from the service and that Thomas forgot the wedding license and walked up the aisle with his pants rolled to protect them from the snow. Born in 1853 in Clinton, Massachusetts, Thomas was a civil engineer of many jobs who occasionally wrote poetry. He was called "Dive" by all his friends. He was quite frank about the name and described himself to his future wife's brother as "the habitué of the dramshop and the turf—the gambling hall and the brothel." Some kind of forced bravado and a need to tell the truth made this often melancholy man state to Annie's father, in an earnest appeal for her hand, that he had been heavily into drink, and worse, but would reform.

Dive did not reform, and in December 1888 Annie Louise, Harold, and a second son, Edwin Tyler (born in 1885 and called Tim), moved to the house of a relative in Norwich, Connecticut. Dive spoke of it with his usual honesty: "The breach is made—it is wide enough and there should be an end of talk." He seldom saw his children before his death on December 5, 1891, in Brooklyn, at 1094 Bergen Street, in the house of his uncle. He died from chronic depression, drink, tuberculosis—or something else so unacceptable that it was only referred to as the fitting result of a life of alcohol and sexual abuse. His sister Jeanie wrote to young Harold: "How near your young father came to being a poet and how handsome and agreeable when sober! What a vehicle rum is for misery and shame." The same sister spoke of the marriage of Annie and Thomas as a frustrated, brilliant match: "Your mother and he were just the wrong too high-spirited rather beautiful-to-see pair to come together."

The father's family was English, originally Welsh, and came to the United States from London in 1832. Bynner's great-grandfather arrived with his seven children—one being Bynner's grandfather Edwin, then sixteen. Also a man of some drink and many jobs—newspaper editor, painter, auctioneer, freight agent, and dealer in brick and lime—Edwin was in 1896 described in *History of the Origin of the Town of Clinton, Massachusetts, 1653–1865* as an important editor of the Clinton *Courant*. The attributes described here would be inherited to a great degree by his poet grandson, Witter.

> Mr. Bynner was a man of literary ability, although he was at times more fluent than a severe taste might demand. He was a man of vivid imagination, keen wit, sound judgement, honest fearlessness and a high ideal of his editorial position. In local affairs, his influence was always used to restrain lawlessness and to promote enterprise. His frequent editorials on such public needs as fire engines, railroads and gas works, on beautifying the Common and planting trees along the streets, and especially on liberality in matters of education by means of school, books and the lecture system, must have had an important influence in the development of the community.

To these qualities should be added that Edwin Bynner married into an old (they arrived in America in 1645) and well-to-do family, the Edgartons of Massachusetts, that he had seven children, and that he was known for his intense belief in democracy and strong feelings against monarchy and slavery. He was also known for his superb ability as a storyteller, an attribute that put him much in demand as a newspaper writer and at public social functions, which frequently included people such as Ralph Waldo Emerson and Louis Agassiz. In Boston in 1870 he had a fatal fall from an omnibus on a winter's night—perhaps he was drunk or drinking—and was spoken of in obituaries in the Boston and New York papers as a man of incomparable qualities of wit, repartee, and mimicry: "Among the rarest and choicest spirits. . . . To secure Bynner for any convivial undertaking was considered almost indispensable—for his presence was an augury of success, as his absence was a precursor of disappointment, if not of failure." It was also noted that he "lacked aim, and persistence, and while conscious of his own powers he yet distrusted their promises." Clearly he was a man of character, ability, nervousness, and mixed directions, as his grandson would be.

One of Edwin's sons was called Edwin Lassetter Bynner, a man who remained a bachelor and lived most of his life in Boston. He was the writer of several popular historical novels on American themes—*Agnes Surriage* (1886) is his best-known work—a fine historian, a poor playwright, and an indifferent lawyer who had received an LL.D. from Harvard Law School. His obituaries by Everett Edward Hale and Barrett Wendell praised his talent as modest and his character as serious and admirable, if singularly lacking in any particularly demonstrative quality that they could portray. He was a quiet, well-bred New England gentleman of the nineteenth-century kind, a rare spirit whose eccentricity and passion were carefully channeled into historical fiction, so far as anyone knew, and whose private life was never recorded even in his letters.

Bynner's mother's side was also unusual. The Brewers were a long established, highly respectable Connecticut family of clergymen, schoolteachers, and, more recently, thriving bankers and businessmen. They appeared to be like the straight, tall elm trees of New England—native and solid—and counted in their past a Chauncy who was the second president of Harvard College, a Bishop Tyler of Norwich, and even the Bushnells of Hartford, one of the most prominent Connecticut families. The Brewers were proud of their independence of spirit and showed a stern frankness in analyzing their own faults and those of others. These people were—and remained, in the poet's mother—headstrong, proper in appearance, and demanding; people who, in their public roles, seemed to have a drive toward respectability, power, and independence.

These qualities never quite came together in their private, intimate selves. One relative is referred to as having misbehaved, appropriately out west, and Annie's father is supposed to have made home life miserable with his private drinking. There is also a family tradition of debilitating stomach illnesses and neuralgic headaches, both of which were inherited by Annie Louise and her son. If the Bynners went in for excessive self-expression, the Brewers sought to hold it back. Writing to her son in 1919, Annie Louise described members of her and her husband's families in the following amusing if also devastating way: "Am alone and was just thinking what a pleasant retrospective—your father a good-for-nothing—drunk—Uncle Walt crazy, Uncle Bob loony, Aunt Sally a flighty irresponsible, Aunt Naome shuffling, Ruth shaking, Aunt Mary Witter senile, Percy a suicide, Hal Witter a suicide, you a pacifist, Tim on the verge of heaven knows what. No wonder I am going to Dr. Dow."

Annie Louise was decidedly the most powerful influence in her son's life. She insisted, and did so relentlessly, that he conduct his life exactly as she wanted. As time went by, Bynner deflected this pressure by regularly distancing himself from her, first through travel and then by going to live in New Hampshire, California, New Mexico, and Mexico, moves she never approved of his making. Santa Fe especially was for her an incomprehensible location, nothing more than a primitive mud heap in the eyes of a woman who lived in New York City in two apartments on the twelfth floor of the Hotel Seymour just off Fifth Avenue on West 45th Street. Strong-willed, opinionated, excessively nervous, often depressed, she was also intelligent and capable and shared with her son an incisive wit that in her case turned most of life into a farce that she attempted to observe from a distance. She suffered many obstacles in life and found few, if any, satisfactory emotional or intellectual outlets—other than her close association with her talented son. Her emotional nature and view of the world influenced him decisively.

≡≡≡

There is an old Bynner family photograph of an elementary school class, grade 4 or 5, posed in front of a school, probably in Connecticut. In the last of four rows, on the right, is young Harold, stepping slightly forward with one shoulder tipped to the camera, hair dark and curly, gaze clear, mouth firmly set but slightly open, the entire face showing a hesitancy and a deliberate assurance that one imagines is created consciously through the efforts of a clever child. It is a handsome face, though the expression is too forced to be convincing.

In the second row on the left side stands the only black child in the all-white group, carefully dressed in dark clothes and hat. She is better dressed than most of her companions and in no way seems ill at ease. Some of her classmates appear to be disheveled and despondent. This photograph is the only indication that Bynner as a child had any early contact with African Americans.

In New York City, after Bynner graduated from Harvard and began to experience the world on his own, he also began to meet African Americans, especially in the early twenties through his friend Carl Van Vechten. Bynner was very interested in the artists and writers and gave Countee Cullen in 1925 and Langston Hughes in 1926 the Witter Bynner Undergraduate Award for poetry, a national award he had established. At a time when few were comfortable in mixed society, Bynner appeared easy in it, and he continued to believe in equality and democracy as essential to the definition of the American experience. He believed in Walt Whitman's democratic America as "the new world," the title of his second volume of poems, published in 1915, a volume concerned with how immigrant and minority groups were reshaping America.

These concerns of Bynner's created the myths that he was Whitman's illegitimate son—born when Whitman was sixty-two—and that Bynner had African American ancestors. Both stories appear to be attempts to explain Bynner's unusual response to democracy and race. It is important to recognize that Bynner came to his commitment to a democratic society from the same narrow limitations of so many Americans of his time. It is a measure of his character that he transcended this narrowness of viewpoint. The measure of how far he came can be seen by contrasting a letter written in 1904 about a visit to North Carolina with his 1944 poem "Defeat," which was published in the *New Republic* and the *New Masses* and in his 1947 volume of verse, *Take Away the Darkness*.

They're a queer lot—irrevocably, I'm convinced, an inferior breed. Southerners bully and verbally abuse them. At first it made me feel uneasy, but now I see that it's the only way to do. Even as it is, they get from three or four niggers service we should think disgustingly slack and deficient in a solitary white servant. . . . Their disenfranchisement is necessary and inevitable. They are an undergrown race—children forever, in every sense but the idealistic—and are fit to be nothing more than servants. And, as I have said, even at that they are inferior.

Defeat

On a train in Texas German prisoners eat
With white American soldiers, seat by seat,
While black American soldiers sit apart,
The white men eating meat, the black men heart.
Now, with that other war a century done,
Not the live North but the dead South has won,
Not yet a riven nation comes awake.

Whom are we fighting this time, for God's sake?
Mark well the token of the separate seat.
It is again ourselves whom we defeat.

≡

In October 1892, Annie Louise, Harold, and Tim moved to Brookline, Massachusetts, to live with Dive's married sister, Jeanie Ernst, a witty, opinionated woman whom Bynner always liked. This period was one of financial difficulties for Mrs. Bynner, who played the piano for a private dancing class and taught at a school in Boston run by Dive's other sister, Caroline Naomi Bynner, a woman of formidable will and intellect, a strict moralist, a spinster, and a great reader of English and French literature. The two sisters felt a strong responsibility to help the busy mother direct Harold and his brother through their early years. The values they instilled must have affected him. Here is Aunt Jeanie writing to the young man:

I look to you to redeem the forfeit of your race. You inherit much good blood—and even better brains from your paternal side—but some deep life errors from both sides of ancestors—weaknesses which you must efface—just be clean and true and all the rest will come—polish your *honor* every day.

Aunt Naomi wrote this to Bynner:

You have a highly nervous organization, inherited from both sides I regret to say—the Bynners were and are all of the fussy petty apprehensive kind. It does no good. Try to down it all. . . . Take better care of your health. Try to live more regularly. You were never vicious, but lawless. All the old Bynners sat up nights and indulged themselves to their hearts' content—and they all had neuralgia.

Bynner's reaction to such pressure was what one might expect. After a dinner one evening with Aunt Naomi, he returned to his room and wrote in his diary: "Was forced for a while to take life as a thing of honor, purpose and character. Much as I love her, I fear there was born in me the lines of a life dishonorable, purposeless and of doubtful character."

In spite of these perceptions of fault in his character—fault so much a part of his family heritage—Bynner was doing well for a young man of seventeen. After four years at Brookline High School, where he was editor of the *Sagamore,* the school literary magazine, Bynner was admitted to Harvard, with aid from the Price Greenleaf Fund. It was 1898, and this heavily pressured young man was eager to prove himself and equally determined to do so in his own way.

———

Like Housman's Shropshire, Harvard became for Bynner a place that expressed the promise of youth. His first book contained a long poem, also used as the book's title, *An Ode to Harvard* (he later changed the title to *Young Harvard*), about a graduate who, returning after four years, remembers what had been so important and beautiful about his college days. Bynner states that no castles in Spain could mean more to him than the turns and turrets of the buildings in the Yard. The poem embraces collegiate emotions we no longer seem to appreciate, but the poem remains a work of deeply felt idealism. From college classes and talks with teachers and students to great football games and quiet evenings, the events of this poem about Harvard represent Bynner's ideal:

> O mean to all those others whom you'll see
> The thousand things in one you mean to me!
>
> O lift forever on the shield of truth,
> Before the armies of mortality,
> The sounding challenge of the spear of youth!

As he says in *An Ode to Harvard,* he was not really interested in his courses, except for some of those in English literature. His study of languages—Greek, Latin, French, and German—was often deficient. Even at this point in his life, he did little that did not interest him directly. He took a course in the history of philosophy with professors George Herbert Palmer and Josiah Royce (grade B-); one in Shakespeare with George Lyman Kittredge (whom he found a frightful dullard and who in return gave him his only C in an English course); one in the drama from 1642 to 1900 with George Pierce Baker (only a B); and one in the philosophy of aesthetics with George Santayana (who awarded Bynner an A-). He graduated with honors in English, although the record is not as brilliant as the talent would suggest. He did what he could do, with an uncritical ease. His Harvard professor Barrett Wendell, who had been a friend of his uncle, the novelist Edwin Lassetter Bynner, wrote on one assignment:

With more than usual sensitiveness to detail, which makes your writing individual and interesting, you are apt to be infirm of literary purpose. That you hand in three sonnets instead of one is typical, I think, of your constitutional disinclination to decision. In consequence, your work is sometimes fastidiously eccentric. Your aim should be assertive strength. Your grade is B. By stronger concentration you may raise it.

The character begins to appear—the open, excessive, all-encompassing lack of discrimination that made him act but frequently led him to excess. He knew he was not free of the past, of its inheritance and its burdens, but he seemed to be striking out against its confining and debilitating concerns without really knowing how or why. His closest friend at college was the poet Arthur Davison Ficke, who referred to Bynner as often found in a state of exhilaration, running "through the yard shrieking, with streaming hair." Bynner accepted that comment as a correct description. An acquaintance took him to task for what was weak in his character and Bynner recorded in his diary: "God help me to eat and walk and sleep regularly, to be silly as little as possible, to like people, to appreciate time and opportunity, to cultivate a sense of duty and not to bury my piece of silver." Bynner was concerned with his friend's lecture to him because he believed it was true, but he could see nothing to do about it beyond saying, "Of course I made resolutions *during* the lecture."

Bynner was the first member of his class to be asked to join the *Advocate,* in March 1900, by its editor, Wallace Stevens: "Pardon my delayed congratulations. Will you prepare a story for your initiation which will take place possibly Thursday next?" Bynner showed his talent and his direction, perhaps more than he intended, in this light piece, later published in the *Advocate,* that carried the heavy title "Revolution":

> Away with that frown from your forehead!
> Away with that storm out there!
> And away with the sign that you've done with your wine!
> Away with you, Emperor Care!

> Here's
> Down with Emperor Care!
> Scorn his command!
> Scoff at his hand!
> Death to Emperor Care!

> Drink deep, and make love, and be merry!
> Of morrows you've wealth to spare.

Oh crink deep, for to-day is fast racing away—
Drink death to you, Emperor Care.

Here's
Death to Emperor Care!
Pluck off his crown!
Drag the fool down!
Death to the Emperor Care!

This solemn pledge to frivolity goes on for three more stanzas and suggests that hidden inside Bynner, perhaps still beyond his self-perception, may have been something related closely to the despair and sickness of his father and grandfather. His clown was a deliberate fool who made fun in order to please the company, who in turn were there to keep the loneliness away. In his folly there was an element of desperation.

Bynner began a "revolution," at least for the males in his family, and in the best way he could conceive. He did not let a progression of circumstances bring him to drink, sickness, and despair, but resolutely heeding his aunts' call to "redeem" his race, he turned the family pattern away from self-reflection and analysis toward high-spirited independence and determined fun. The price one pays for such a deliberate act of will is a certain loss of the self, a shutting away of the pain and with it serious self-reflection. It is unlikely that at this point Bynner even knew what he was doing. He simply chose what seemed the best possible course. He had then and throughout his life virtually no interest in sustained philosophical inquiry, and he had a blatant hostility to psychological analysis. It is as if the analytical process were quite alien to his brilliant, sharp, emotive, and playful being.

For Bynner, the life of the college was in the fun he had and the romance he saw everywhere around him. Stoughton 3 was his room for four years, and it was "hung solid with framed photographs of painting, sculpture, architecture, or classic ruins, and on the mantle family photographs." There was a grate for a coal fire, and no running water, except from a pump in the Yard. Just above him lived English professor Charles Townsend Copeland, and Bynner's habitually late hours, booming voice, and high shrieking laughter necessitated endless scenes with "Copey" and in the dean's office. The famous Mr. Copeland was patient and good-natured, but Bynner was insatiable. He liked to get up at 2:00 in the morning, assemble friends for buckwheat cakes and ginger ale at Rammy's, a local eatery on Harvard Square, and return for more talk and laughter. He formed a club of about ten friends to read Meredith's novels.

The group included Arthur Ficke, George Claire St. John, the future headmaster of the Choate School, and Karl Young, later to be professor of English at Wisconsin and Yale. These readings also resulted in noise— at one, Bynner, after drinking a tankard of beer, could not stop talking— but out of this love of Meredith came an essay, "George Meredith's Style," that won Bynner second prize in the 1902 Bowdoin contest for the best literary essay. The Boylston Prize for Elocution (second place) also went to him that year.

Unlike the interests of the typical gentleman-athlete of the time, the type of student most admired at the college, Bynner's interests lay seriously in the arts. He went repeatedly into Boston to the theater, especially to see Minnie Maddern Fiske, to the opera, where he was a "super," and to the symphony. He would frequently end such evenings at Marliave's, a restaurant with a bohemian character he enjoyed. He taught French to a class of one—"a man 45 with a mustache"—at the Prospect Union, an early Harvard version of extension education. He became involved with the suffrage movement. After a speech he made in 1901 in Brookline, a woman said to Bynner's mother, "You must be very proud of your son," to which she replied with frankness and pleasure, "You don't know him." He wrote in his diary that Wallace Stevens's high spirits one evening at Rammy's prompted Stevens to leap the counter in mock rape of the waitress, landing both of them in a heap on the floor. A professor was present who reported him, and this event led to Stevens's early departure from Harvard.

Bynner became "Hal" during these college years, lost the election for college poet, 296 to 76, and on November 24, 1901, reported in his journal on an early sexual encounter: "Last night I made new friends in strange rooms. After walking alone from Marliave's to City Hall, I boarded what I knew as a car because it had a yellow curl on its forehead and pink silk underdrawers." At dinner one evening with George Santayana, Bynner, with the audacity he enjoyed showing, asked the cautious, aesthetic Spaniard if he was in love with anyone. The philosopher stared at him coldly and solemnly answered, "One moon has she, and another not yet risen." When writing the poems in *An Ode to Harvard* a few years later, Bynner described Santayana as the

> Spanish poet-philosopher whose eye would so beguile
> That you'd see no more his meaning, but the flaring altar-oil
> That was burning as for worshippers inside

When Bynner graduated in 1902, his Aunt Naomi wrote to him about his future and his responsibilities. She reminded him that he was the first-born in a family that had a great sense of its importance and propriety, and it was up to him to carry on the family and its best traditions. Also, he had lived in a female-dominated world with a male heritage that was deeply deficient. He was without money and would continue to be, yet was expected to be respectable in his life-style. She accepted his interest in literature, provided what he wrote was proper and correct.

He was being asked to carry forward into the world a tradition for which there would be little place. Aunt Naomi looked to a past that was not without its great faults and in any case no longer existed. Her New England and Anglo-Saxon order would no longer prevail in a world that was to consist largely of new immigrants from countries with other religions and different values. Bynner could see that this old tradition was not adapting to the future. He never lost certain New England qualities—his Harvard accent, his democratic good manners, his easy directness, his appearance of self-assurance—but he spent his life seeking a path that would move him away from the narrow standards of his family and its New England restrictions and into a world that reflected the more diverse and complicated elements in his nature and his country. In him one sees the transformation of the New England sensibility from its place at the center of American culture to its position as only a part of the larger, more complex cultural milieu that was to exist in the twentieth century.

Bynner's mother had remarried, which was to bring a change in the family's finances. Her new husband, Walter Liveridge Wellington, was a successful and wealthy businessman, rather simple in manner, and very generous, a man who had been like a relative: his first wife, Sarah, had been engaged to the brother of Bynner's father; this brother died of smallpox with Sarah tending him; she then married Wellington and died young herself. Wellington, who was said to have been with Bynner's father when he died, married Annie Louise Bynner in December 1901 and moved with her to a splendid house on St. Mark's Avenue in Brooklyn. Unfortunately, he, like Bynner's father, also suffered from extreme depression. He was institutionalized and died in 1914. His daughter, Ruth, whom Annie Louise raised, had multiple sclerosis, became addicted to drugs and alcohol, and died in 1919, having caused many painful problems for Bynner's mother over the years. In spite of all her difficulties, Ruth Wellington was able to elicit great love from her adopted family. When she died, she left a substantial legacy to her stepmother and a small inheritance to Bynner and his brother, Tim.

For a man of his age—twenty-one in 1902—and his time, Bynner had traveled extensively: from Brooklyn through all of New England and some of New York state, into Canada as far north as Quebec City, to Buffalo, to Chicago to visit college friends and his Palmer relatives, and to Davenport, Iowa, to see Arthur Ficke and his family. Upon graduation, he expected to stay on at Harvard to teach English, but Mr. Wellington, with Annie Louise's encouragement, proposed a tour of Europe and then a return to New York for a year's try at business. The proposal suited everyone, especially Bynner, who had been uncertain about his choice of teaching. An interview was arranged at *McClure's* magazine in July, a position was promised him to start in October upon his return, and he then sailed to Europe on the S.S. *Philadelphia*.

His grand tour started in London. He crossed the Channel to Mont-Saint-Michel, Amiens, Beauvois, Paris, Versailles, Chartres, Geneva, Heidelberg, the Rhine, Hamburg, and Amsterdam, came back to London, Cambridge, Lincoln, Melrose Abbey, Edinburgh, Stratford, and Oxford, and set sail from Southampton on September 13.

Bynner called London "a larger and older Boston where nobody spits." He made notes about his travels that illustrate his perception and wit and his quick, often unreflective mind.

London:
Women and children at bars late at night.
Gamins in twos and threes, arms locked, singing popular songs.
Women of high color and reddish or muddy yellow hair accost you
    shrilly on street in grotesque costume—inviting in all but appearance.
"Don't notice their English—it's American."

France:
The people stare, then melt indoors.
Real Madonnas with living babies.
Amiens Cathedral with spires would be the Venus de Milo with arms.
The urinals at Caen are the most exposed yet.
Two peasants (Beauvois to Compiègne) lean out windows six trains
    apart and conduct genial and easy conversation all the way.
Spoken French is one grand nasal elision.

Germany:
Germans and Dutch must be scrupulous door-shutters; the sign is
    ubiquitous, "The door closes itself."
Conscious ruins on the Rhine.

> Germans speak better English than French.
>
> A German on the Rigi train—from Hamburg by his coat—bought four bunches of black cherries and gave me one of the bunches. Our only way of friendly communication when we saw each other on the boat was to show our black tongues.

The supreme moment of his travel came on September 3, when Bynner went to Box Hill, Surrey, to meet George Meredith, the elderly novelist and poet, a man by then quite deaf and immobile—Bynner says he no longer had the use of his legs. Bynner's three literary gods were Meredith, Whitman, and A. E. Housman. He described them as "an odd but complementary trio: the patrician self, the democratic self, the ascetic self." Of these he was to meet only Meredith, although he corresponded briefly with Housman. Years later, in 1956, Bynner took his notes of this meeting and wrote "A Young Visit with George Meredith."

> On leaving the train at Box Hill, I felt my heart fiddling and thumping. Could a man just of age experience in the 1950's any such tremors, on any such pilgrimage, as those that stirred me on mine at the turn of the century? Are young men of today, about to meet Picasso, Malraux, or Stravinsky, as shaken by such excitement? The younger generation seems cool today. Perhaps younger generations always seem cool. Several times along the walk from the station I stopped to make sure that the person moving was I. My heart was not only in my throat but in my ears, half-deafening me as I approached the presence of one who, to his disciple, was a supreme being in the heaven of letters. The sensation returned and then slowly subsided on my train trip back to London, during which a still hypnotized hand managed to draw from my brief case a black-and-white checkered notebook with a Spencerian label, *Compositions,* and joggle into it paragraphs remembered from the afternoon. Echoes of Meredith's voice made for me a recording in that book, as actual voices were later to do on discs.

Europe impressed Bynner and intrigued him but never for a moment convinced him that its civilization was more interesting or important than his own. If Henry James, Ezra Pound, T. S. Eliot, and the group of Americans in Paris in the twenties felt a need for European manners and culture in order to find themselves, Bynner simply did not. As he grew older, the failure of Europeans to understand Whitman's new world left Bynner indifferent and, at times, impatient. He did not return to Europe for almost fifty years. He went west and then on to Asia. It was his love of the Southwest and especially of Asia that seriously affected his poetry, and it was this influence especially that increasingly left him outside the mainstream of modern verse and its criticism. He came to believe that the elements of culture were far more than European and much more diverse than his New England and Protestant sensibility imagined. He was, early in the century, and quite genuinely, interested in the diversity of cultures.

≡≡≡

In 1902 Bynner began his New York and *McClure's* journal this way, and in doing so clearly dramatized his chaotic and brilliant nature:

October 6: My first day in business—and I refrained from writing a letter on McClure paper: I'm growing older. My tastes don't frighten me as much as they make me realize how little method and dispatch in clerical matters Harvard training has given me.

October 8: Met William Aspenwall Bradley [later the well-known literary agent in Paris], who compiles circulars, and S. S. McClure. New duties confusing and difficult.

October 14: At the office my dazed activity is losing the adjective. The mists are rising.

October 20: Saturday the cashier handed me as I went out, two little envelopes. Castles began to show fantastic turrets in the air.

October 23: I have been given the combination that opens the safe!

November 7: Remembered after dining with W. Morrow that the safe was open, went back at 10:15 in dark elevator to shut it. (Later convinced Sister Ruth that I am insane. Am I?)

November 17: A very good day at the office. All of a sudden I seem to know the ropes better than I did last week or yesterday.

November 18: A quatrain which I wrote yesterday to show Molly Best that I can do a "McClurish po'm" is accepted for the January number. It was written as a parody.

He became the poetry editor and an accomplished editor of fiction. Once, at McClure's instructions, Bynner cut a Willa Cather story to everyone's satisfaction but Miss Cather's; her wrath was so great that McClure refused to accept the responsibility and said it was done on Bynner's own initiative. Bynner saved an O. Henry story from rejection and got him as a regular writer for *McClure's*. The two became close friends, dining around town, taking walks, talking literature. O. Henry's letters to Bynner are full of light, warm fun and constant requests for a loan. Once O. Henry repaid a loan with the manuscripts of three short stories. Bynner sold them in the twenties for cash to build a second floor onto his house in Santa Fe; for many years he called it "the O. Henry Story."

Bynner lunched, dined, and went to the theater and opera, both constant amusements, with many of the writers and artists who came to *McClure's*, to the publishing firm of McClure, Phillips, or to the Players, the theatrical and literary club in Gramercy Park that Bynner joined in 1903 and generally used as his New York focus and address. The list of his companions is large and catholic: Henry Harland, the fastidious expatriate American who wrote romances of European royalty and edited in London the notorious publication *The Yellow Book;* Barry Faulkner, the muralist and a Harvard classmate; Augustus Saint-Gaudens and his son Homer, also a classmate; Richard Watson Gilder, the genteel editor of the *Century;* the poet Richard Le Gallienne, who introduced Bynner to Housman's work and praised Bynner's poetry; Rex Beach, the writer of Alaskan adventure stories who spat regularly behind the couch in the Players during a lunch Bynner arranged; the artist Rockwell Kent; the playwright Percy MacKaye; the novelist Booth Tarkington; John Sloan and Robert Henri and the other painters of the Ashcan School who came to New York over the next few years; Mark Twain, whom Bynner often visited late at night at 21 Fifth Avenue, enjoying his writing and delighting in his Rabelaisian humor; John Dewey, with whom he marched up Fifth Avenue for women's rights; and Bynner's antithesis—Henry James.

The two were an odd couple. Bynner respected James's refinements but also found them excessive and amusing; Bynner's youth and charm were delightful to James, but Bynner never offered his writing as a critical issue for the Jamesian mind. They saw a good deal of one another in 1905 in New York, especially at the Players, where they would lunch and then go for walks.

In 1905 Bynner was allowed by the Master to publish a memoir of their conversations, in interview form—a great concession on James's part—and Bynner returned once again to their relationship in an article he wrote in 1943. Bynner, showing respectful amusement, called the first article "A Word or Two with Henry James" and went on to print a several-column recollection of James's nonstop sentences and paragraphs. These paragraphs are like an early draft of James's chapter on New York that appeared in 1907 in *The American Scene,* his book about his visit here in 1904–1905. James talks about the loss of the past, the recollection of it in the old buildings in Gramercy Park, and his excited remembrance of the theater as a child: "I was seated in the theatre with my eyes on the old green curtain, feeling quite convinced that in a few minutes before that curtain should rise, I was doomed to be removed by accident or death or some unforeseen punishment." The accuracy of Bynner's reporting of the Jamesian dialogue is suggested by this revealing paragraph on Boston:

> After the shock of New York in those one or two hot days, I was glad to be back again in Boston, the city with the charm exclusively its own. Its distinction is, of course, its oneness, its completeness, its homogeneity, qualities it has retained almost precisely as it had them when I was a boy, and it was a rural, or rather a rustic city, the conservative, collective and representative capital of New England. One feels, to be sure, the disadvantages of such advantage. Boston's standard of comparison is bounded entirely by its own precincts. It is given to bidding you to swan and setting you goose. But this very stiffness, stuffiness, this very inaccessibility to a breath of outer air, produces, in however close an atmosphere, a demeanor of self-respect and of patrician dignity.

Bynner and James never saw one another again, although they occasionally wrote, but Bynner's portrait of James in these two published sketches remains an accurate record of the Master in his late, ripe, brilliant style. Of course, Bynner seems to have missed, or little valued, the entire issue that so preoccupied James—the character of the American in relation to the European and the American's emergence at center stage of modern life. An obsession for James, this role of the American was something that Bynner assumed was his birthright, or else he was not analytical enough to consider it at all. Bynner never felt a need to believe the European was superior or any kind of threat. The European was merely older and different, and nowhere as interesting to Bynner as the Native American, the Hispanic, or the Asian. Such a view of the world was, in essence, about as far as one could get from Henry James's view.

Bynner's life in New York also included the Yeatses. Bynner saw most often the father, John Butler Yeats, because he lived in New York and was part of the same circle that met at Petipas, a small boarding house and restaurant at 317 West 29th Street run by three French sisters as a rendezvous for artistic people. A dinner in the garden there was painted by John Sloan in 1910 with John Butler Yeats at the head of the table, Dolly and John Sloan, the poet Alan Seeger, the critic Van Wyck Brooks, and several others. Sloan reported that he took John Butler Yeats to his first baseball game on July 28 and celebrated that evening at Petitpas his wife Dolly's birthday. On August 2 he began the painting from memory of this evening. Bynner also knew John Butler Yeats's son, the poet William Butler Yeats, and his artist brother, Jack, and John Quinn, the American lawyer who so expertly supported the Yeatses and the cause of

Irish and American writers and artists and who created one of the earliest and best collections of modern paintings before his death in 1924. Sometime around 1908 Quinn entertained the group, and Bynner later in life described the occasion:

> I met William Butler Yeats first, I think, with his father at John Quinn's, and Jack Yeats, his brother, the painter, was there, the two younger presences feeling like a white swan and a black duck, the father more like a gray phoenix. As to Quinn, among his modernistic paintings, in spite of the coalish beard under his skin, his face and head, posed in a stiff white collar which seemed at the same time too large and too tight for him, looked like a calla lily in a milk-glass vase. Quinn was emphatic, a bit feverish, the Yeats family like something he was dreaming. It was an Armory Show all in itself.

At Bynner's request, Quinn asked William Butler Yeats to send a comment on *An Ode to Harvard and Other Poems,* which Bynner used in promoting the book. It seems a rather evasive and hesitant remark: "Judging by what I have read you have the control of a powerful, eloquent, vehement language and thought that rushes on impetuous to its sentient end and I thank you for sending me the book."

Bynner's remarkable memory is shown in another literary encounter that took place in April 1904. This time it was with the young Wallace Stevens. These two Harvard friends and poets, rivals who went separate ways in literature, recorded the following sequence of events in the journal each kept of his early years in New York.

Bynner:
April 8: In evening at the Francis drank with Wallace Stevens till we were drunk. We slept hard in his room.

April 9: Stevens is not only likeable but a wholesome friend—particularly as antidote to chatter-brains with tenderer manners. Through being much alone, he has gone daffy a little. His egotism is monumental. My intrusion with an egotism of my own confused him by not wholly displeasing him. It was the same in Cambridge.

Stevens:
April 9: Strange phantasmagoria! Bynner, the old *Advocate* poet, dropped in on me last night & I went with him to the Cafe Francis in West 35th Street where we sat & smoked & talked & drank St. Estèphe until after midnight. An inexplicable fellow—the manner of a girl, the divination, flattery & sympathy of a woman, the morbid-

ness & reverie of a poet, the fire and enthusiasm & ingenuousness of a young man. He has gathered his own impressions & odd ones they are. Has he passed safely through the sentimental, sketchy stage?

Bynner:
April 14: Wallace Stevens shows me, in his irregular comment of a journal, what he has written about our reacquaintance. Liking and admiring him, I pretty well memorized what he wrote of me. "Strange phantasmagoria! I met Bynner, the poet of *Advocate* days. He is an inexplicable fellow, has the manners of a girl; the divination, sympathy and flattery of a woman; the morbidness and reverie of a poet; the enthusiasm, fire and ingenuousness of a young man. He has derived his own impressions and they are original ones. Is he, perhaps, only coming through the sketchy stage?"
    April 15: He has so much more to say about me than I about him that I was more pleased with the fact than vexed with details.

Stevens:

(May?) 1904
Dear Hal: Last week my insides were in great disorder—I was, indeed, sick with a sickness. But by dint of going to bed at eight, & of much sitzbathing, & dieting & lithia-ing & porous plastering, I am knocking about again. My bar exams are on June 7 & until then I intend to apply myself most conscientiously to grinding. Therefore our congeniality must ex necessitate be a thing apart from "drink" (as you call it—hideously). In fact, I detest rum, & never intended that, if we were to see much of one another, there should be much liquor spilled. It is a tiresome thing. My idea of life is a fine evening, an orchestra & a crowd *at a distance,* a medium dinner, a glass of something cool & at the same time wholesome, & a soft, full Panatela. If that is congenial to you, we can surely arrange it after June 7—unless I flunk. In the meantime we must be without much ceremony, although eager enough.

The sequence is a rare revelation of two personalities more through what it implies than through what it says. As men and poets they were and remained at a great distance. Stevens continued to look with skepticism on Bynner. Bynner spoke with guarded admiration of Stevens, yet advised Alfred Knopf not to bother to publish his poems. The two poets could never be close, but they wrote each other over the years and near the end of their lives became less reserved with one another. It is as if, in spite of their differences, their memory of the past gave them something important to share in their old age. Yet Stevens could never see why Bynner went to Santa Fe and Bynner never understood how anyone could choose to live in Hartford, Connecticut!

<hr>

Once he was at *McClure's,* it never occurred to Bynner to leave and return to Harvard to teach, although he had to struggle to make himself fit into this professional office. Clearly Mr. McClure liked him and respected his work; the uncertainty was in Bynner. Early in 1903 he began to suffer from extreme neuralgic headaches that lasted for days and continued to occur intermittently throughout the year. "Daily the wild pain circling like an acid round my eye unhinges my hope and care of the world." When he returned to his office after several days at home, his first remark in his journal was this: "Wheels at the office are smoother and smoother in their round. The rub now is to establish a conviction that I'm solid and to make myself popular. I can do the first if I'll say little and look a lot—but the latter, how?"

Interestingly, Bynner was able to convey an elegant and finely social exterior, at least to certain people in the literary world. This contrast in how he was perceived would continue throughout his life: he could be seen, as he often thought he was, as undisciplined and excessive, or he could be seen as Jessie Rittenhouse described him, during this period, in her autobiography, *My House of Life:*

> And what company would have been complete without the charm and *savoir-faire* of Witter Bynner? Tall, svelte, with that air which in Victorian days would have been called elegance, he had to a marked degree the grace of social contact. Nor was this in any sense a mere social acquirement; no one was more spontaneously sincere. He had the good fortune to be *simpatico* with many people because he liked and understood them, and who can fail to respond to this particular type of friendliness? He radiated youth and conviction that life is good.

The true state of his emotions is clearly reflected in his journal, which he kept in this brief style and only sporadically. These remarks indicate what his life in New York was like as he maintained his external social manner but seemed unable to determine what he might do with his often excessive and undisciplined nature and talent.

1903

July 28: Letters from the Henry Harlands, one introducing me to E. C. Stidman

Lapse to August 9: At Hammerstein's Roof Garden an actor took a shine to me and would have had me drink with him except for Jimmie Fraser

August 10: 22 Years old and growing used to New York. Soon I shall be one of the damned who like it and know only work and diversion—no peace.

August 11: Life in the office begins to be a daily need. I long over Sunday to be back in harness.

1904

April 16: Last night, from a long talk with Barry [Faulkner], I walked home in a chattering chill, to arrive at our door in Marlborough Arms with no government of my legs and a general dimness as to the world. "I'm not drunk," I said to Homer, "I'm sick." He put me to bed, where I writhed in pain all night.

April 17: When Homer telephoned mother at 6 a.m. she was dressed and ready. She had wakened Uncle Walt at 2:30—the hour, Homer says, when I came home—and told him of a vivid dream. The bell at 853 St. Mark's had rung, she had risen and gone to the door, opened it and found me slumped to my knees saying, "I'm not drunk. I'm sick." In spite of Uncle Walt she had dressed and was ready. Strange telepathy, like Uncle Ned Bynner's. I was limp after acute pain of rheumatism in legs, from which only the doctor's morphine relieved me. I hadn't been able to stay still an instant till with the morphine I went a bit out of my head.

1905

June 2: The day wasn't bad—very little gout and no head. I think I pounded it down last night by chop suey and rice and tea, which I consumed at 3 a.m. with my eyes shut. Five flights at the Marlborough Arms appalling me, I chose rather to circle twenty blocks and regain strength. On the circuit I saw a white paper in the gutter and, leaning against a lamp-post, wrote a poem on it.

His constant associations with all kinds of people in endless entertainments, his breezy, jaunty personality, his many excursions to dinner, the theater, and the opera, his frantic pace in everything, his heavy drinking, and his attempts at the same time to write—all these revealed or disguised a deep uncertainty about his direction and an inability to give of himself fully to anyone or anything. His family consisted of an increasingly dominating mother, another weak and decaying father, a younger brother trying to settle himself in the cotton business, and a brilliant and pathetically mad stepsister. Bynner needed to know who he was, to decide how he should move, and also to reach into himself to find his own voice. To know that he was a poet of lyric grace and simplicity, a lonely extrovert and clown hiding his love for men in a garrulous affection for mankind—this perception was still far beyond him. Now he could go only as far as this remark on May 19, 1903: "Will Bradley is off on his honeymoon. He'll not be separate anymore—not happily and boyishly so. I'm afraid girls strike me as an exotic diversion or else an exotic intrusion." When he considered that in a year or so Homer Saint-Gaudens and he might live together in New York, which they briefly did, Bynner wrote in his journal, "God grant that I may by that time be a wholesome chap whom he shall continue to like." He says of another college friendship, "But why should I expect anyone to value my friendship? In all conscience I have little to give." His uncertainty about himself, his hunger for affection and respect, his inability to commit himself personally, were marking him.

In all of this, there is not yet any direct acknowledgment of his homosexuality, but the foregoing remarks suggest that Bynner was aware that his relationship to men had another and deeply compelling quality. The tension that existed already in this highly sensitive character could only be augmented by a growing awareness of his sexual attraction to men, an awareness that would emerge clearly in the next few years.

In October 1906 he finally left *McClure's*. He wanted to escape his mother and her pressures, leave New York and the excessiveness that it seemed to compel in him, and devote himself to writing. He went to live in the house of Homer and Carlotta Saint-Gaudens, in Cornish, New Hampshire. Cornish was a summer community for well-to-do New Yorkers and Bostonians who were interested in the arts, and it included important and respectable artists such as Augustus Saint-Gaudens, Maxfield Parrish, and Kenyon Cox and writers such as Percy MacKaye, the playwright, and Herbert Croly, the editor of the *New Republic* and author of *The Promise of American Life*. Bynner had arranged to rent a study and bedroom from Homer and Carlotta and to pay for board. Beginning with this departure from New York, his life now began a pattern of regular withdrawals, movements away from what he felt were disturbances; these retreats never completely worked, for he always brought with him what was disturbing him, but for the moment they gave him release and time to write.

It was while staying in Cornish that Bynner became deeply engaged in the women's suffrage movement. Since college he had been interested in suffrage and had continued his involvement, including leading the men's section of the first parade on Fifth Avenue on May 6, 1911, marching with John Dewey and George Middleton. Ten thousand women (including Bynner's mother and stepsister) and one hundred men were in the parade, and Bynner said the men were "greeted by multitudinous howls of derision and hate all along its course." It is difficult to imagine the anger and confusion caused by women's suffrage and its related social issues. Harvard refused a hall to let the suffragette Mrs. Pankhurst speak to the undergraduate suffrage league and would not let Radcliffe women hear an anti-child labor lecture for fear it would radicalize their thinking. Bynner traveled all over the state to organize the league in New Hampshire in preparation for the vote. All this was so stimulating that it acted as the catalyst to focus his thinking and his writing. He records the process in his journal for 1911 in what is an unusually revealing statement.

> Abolition of all that oppresses and estranges is the aim which has for its constructive work the establishment of unity. Every artifice of inequality and privilege must be broken down. At last explanation came of my belief in Equal Suffrage, in trusting people with their own affairs. Responsibility means eventual understanding. . . . There is a thrill in finding one's scattered ardors related to the creative vision. At college and in New York I cared more than was suspected for democratic matters. Equal Suffrage, as a matter of justice, always stirred and summoned me. Lately I have learned why. Discovering my God to be finally evolved and conjoined beauty of life, I have seen that we are ourselves God in process. As long as I believed in an absolute Power above and beyond life, I could not feel the necessity for human endeavor. . . . Friends complain that, giving so much time to Suffrage I am neglecting my work. I only wish I could give more time to it until a breach has been made among the Eastern States. To live poetry is the best way to write it. My inner assurance that the more I live by my faith the better I shall write by it reassures me as to my friends' eventual satisfaction.

It is a projection, but not one that appears excessive, to see this statement as equally applicable to Bynner's emerging homosexuality. The sexual freedom and the freedom of choice that make an individual aware and responsible are what he sought for women and for himself. It is also possible to see how the statement applies to Bynner's growing and intense commitment to a type of democracy in America to which Whitman led him—the inclusive and generous world of diverse and independent people relishing their differences and living openly with them.

Harold Witter Bynner as he appeared at age three in 1884 while living in Brooklyn, New York. Bynner is referred to hereafter as "WB." All photographs are from the Houghton Library, Harvard University.

WB poses with his classmates, likely when he was eight or nine and living in Norwich, Connecticut. He is in the last row, fourth from the right.

WB at age thirteen showing the good looks and charm he was always to possess.

WB, his mother Anne Louise (1858–1937), and his
brother Edwin Tyler (1855–1959), called Tim. WB was
almost thirteen when this photograph was taken in
June 1894 in Brookline.

With a slight wisp of moustache,
WB graduated in 1889 from
Brookline High School. He is
seventeen in this picture and on
his way to Harvard.

In 1907 WB moved to Cornish, New Hampshire
and rented a room from Homer St. Gaudens
(1880–1958) and his wife Carlotta. The house is
just up the hill from the home and studio of
Augustus St. Gaudens (1848–1907). Bynner
stands at the door of the house with Carlotta,
center, and a friend.

This interior photograph shows the study in Cornish that was WB's main place of work from 1905 to 1917.

Throughout his life, WB was seriously interested in photography and knew many important photographers. This portrait was made by Arnold Genthe (1869–1942), likely in San Francisco in 1912 on WB's first trip to the West Coast.

One of a series of publicity photographs taken around 1913–1914 when WB was making many speaking trips across the country.

Refusing to serve in the military, WB agreed to go to the University of California at Berkeley in 1918 to teach voice to those in the Students Auxiliary Training Corps. Here he instructs a young student in Berkeley's Greek Theater.

WB and Kiang Kang-hu (1893–1954), his co-translator for *The Jade Mountain*, met in 1918 in Berkeley and spent eleven years on the translation.

WB and Ficke at a temple in Japan.

On WB's first trip to Asia in 1917 he spent his time mainly with Arthur Ficke (1893–1945) and his first wife Evelyn (1880–1954). They went to Japan, Korea, and China. On the second trip in 1920–21, Bynner traveled to China and made acquaintances there, both American and Chinese. Again, Arthur Ficke and his wife were with him.

WB with a great Buddha in Japan.

WB with Ho Chi, his rickshaw man in Peking, a good friend on both visits.

33

WB astride a camel; note that he is wearing spats.

One of WB's young guides who was able to show him aspects of Chinese life not easily accessible to the usual tourist.

WB was often to affect a Chinese style after his extended trips to that country. Here he is in 1918 in his rooms in the Hotel Carlton in Berkeley.

If the struggle for direction was resolving in his mind to some degree, it was only just beginning to do so. The other pressure was there in the form of this letter of July 1911 from Aunt Naomi. While in itself amusing, its insensitive demands for conformity must have been frustrating to Bynner, who was struggling for so much more.

It is now five years since you resigned your regular position—quit regular employment to devote yourself to the writing of a play. You haven't succeeded yet in doing it. Do you still think you can, or that you have the kind of talent requisite for the production of a play?

Your little lyrics are very pretty. Many of them quite beautiful but will the production of them satisfy you as a life work? Do you feel that you have been developed? Advanced?

Between 1907, when he left New York, and 1915, when he published his second book of verse, his creative life was eclectic, as if he were experimenting with the many elements of established and especially popular cultures. He published his first book in 1907, *An Ode to Harvard and Other Poems;* he wrote *Kit,* a one-act play, and *The Mechanic,* a full-length play, with Cecil B. DeMille, but nothing developed for Bynner with either piece; he wrote several other one-act plays, three in verse, which had a few productions—one of these, *Tiger,* on prostitution, received considerable publicity; he tried dramatizing some novels and translated an Italian farce; he wrote songs and attempted a musical version of *Everyman,* called *Anygirl;* he translated *Iphigenia in Taurus* for Isadora Duncan, who performed parts of it before her theater was closed down. His next book, *The New World* (1915), was a Whitmanesque song in praise of the new America.

His two books of poems during this period, *An Ode to Harvard* and *The New World,* show Bynner reaching out for ideas that could establish order in his personal and poetic worlds. What is important in the first is its lyric quality and its traditional themes of nature, youth, beauty, and death, themes to which he would often return in his poetry. In the second, Bynner focuses upon his passionate commitment to the democratic experience of this country. Each contains something more difficult for us to appreciate today—Bynner's movement away from the remote and romantic idealism of the past to a vision that he saw as more contemporary, real, and even "popular." He himself said of the *Ode:* "Apart from my other verse, I take a defiant sort of pride in the *Ode,* feeling it to be of the poetry of today concerned with real things. I am hoping that you will find in it not mere pleasantry, but a sincere expression of worthier material than is to be found in the more conventionally poetical pieces preferred by some of the critics." The interesting point of *The New World* is that part of it was originally delivered as the Phi Beta Kappa address at Harvard in 1911 as "An Immigrant." It reflects Bynner's growing awareness of the changing America that was taking shape around him, the new order he saw coming into existence as the vast immigrant population took its place in America and set the tempo for the new century. Certainly part of Bynner's confusion at this time was his serious effort to integrate the many new and diverse elements of his culture into some meaningful pattern and not just allow his writing to be a product of a mere conventional and narrow past.

Using as his muse in *The New World* a figure named Celia, based upon a writer friend of Bynner's, Herselia A. Mitchell-Keays, he invokes the spirit of Whitman to lead the soul of the nation to unity. It is easy to question the style and syntax of the poem, but it is important to recognize that the ideal being expressed is exceedingly generous and democratic for its day and not even commonplace in a much later time. Bynner was marching to the different drummer of Emerson, Thoreau and Whitman and was to make this democratic expression a central part of his life and work.

> There was a poet Celia loved, who hearing all around
> The multitudinous tread
> Of common majesty,
> Made of the gathering insurgent sound
> Another continent of poetry.
> His name is writ in his blood, mine and yours.
> . . . "And when he celebrates
> These States,"
> She said, "how can Americans worth their salt
> But listen to the wavesong on their shores,
> The waves and Walt,
> And hear the windsong over rock and wood,
> The winds and Walt,
> And let the mansong enter at their gates
> And know that it is good!"
>
> > Walt Whitman, by his perfect friendliness
> Has let me guess
> That into Celia, into me,
> He and unnumbered dead have come
> To be our intimates,

To make of us their home,
Commingling earth and heaven . . .
That by our true and mutual deed
We shall at last be shriven
Of these hypocrisies and jealous creeds
And petty separate fates—
That I in every man and he in me,
Together making God, are gradually creating whole
The single soul . . .
        Somebody called Walt Whitman—
Dead!
He is alive instead,
Alive as I am. When I lift my head,
His head is lifted. When his brave mouth speaks,
My lips contain his word. And when his rocker creaks
Ghostly in Camden, there I sit in it and watch my hand grow old
And take upon my constant lips the kiss of younger truth . . .
It is my joy to tell and to be told
That he in all the world and me,
Cannot be dead,
That I, in all the world and him, youth after youth
Shall lift my head.

≡≡≡

  During this time, in order to earn money, Bynner began to lecture extensively throughout the United States, sometimes on suffrage, sometimes on poetry. His lectures, which took him to every part of the country, his plays, his criticism, and his numerous poems in periodicals made him one of the bright young names in literature in America. Bynner was often referred to along with Amy Lowell, Carl Sandburg, Vachel Lindsay, and Edna St. Vincent Millay as representing the new and diverse American voices.

  Bynner was an important part of this group of American poets. His reputation was growing, and his direction seemed established. It is typical of Bynner that the moment he became part of something, he felt a need to separate himself. This need to separate himself from an established pattern was illustrated dramatically in 1916 in the hoax he and Arthur Ficke created that became known as the Spectra Hoax. Under the guise of humor and playful deception, Bynner, who originated the idea, set himself against the poets of the time, and in doing so he created great uncertainty about himself and his poetry among contemporary poets and critics. It is as though, having been badly deceived once, they would never quite be willing to trust and include him again. Yet it is also true that with the Spectra poems Bynner began for the first time to find his own voice in poetry. The freedom to write under an assumed name released him.

Bored with all the current "schools" of poetry, especially the Imagism of Amy Lowell and Ezra Pound, Bynner made up a new school called Spectrism, to illustrate how anyone could create a school of poetry. He explained that Spectrism tried to see the spectre in our life and capture the varied light of the spectrum. The theory is tenuous but was just convincing enough to be believable in a day when everyone was trying the new and was afraid of rejecting it. Bynner became Emanuel Morgan and Ficke became Anne Knish, both reputedly from Pittsburgh, but with European backgrounds. They published their poems in all the important, small magazines, and their work was seriously praised by some of the best critics. The poems never contained titles but were referred to as "Opus 40" or "Opus 72" and did not appear in any order. The first poem here is by Ficke and the others by Bynner.

Anne Knish

Opus 118
If bathing were a virtue, not a lust,
I would be dirtiest.

> To some, housecleaning is a holy rite.
For myself, houses would be empty
But for the golden motes dancing in sunbeams.

> Tax-assessors frequently overlook valuables.
Today they noted my jade.
But my memory of you escaped them.

Emanuel Morgan

Opus 40
Two cocktails round a smile,
        A grapefruit after grace,
Flowers in an aisle
        . . . Were your face.

A strap in a street-car,
        A sea-fan on the sand,

A beer on a bar
        . . . Were your hand.

The pillar of a porch,
        The tapering of an egg,
The pine of a torch
        . . . Were your leg—

Sun on the Hellespont,
        White swimmers in the bowl
Of the baptismal font
        Are your soul.

Opus 104
How terrible to entertain a lunatic!
To keep his earnestness from coming close!

A Madagascar land-crab once
Lifted blue claws at me
And rattled long black eyes
That would have got me
Had I not been gay.

Opus 6
If I were only dafter
        I might be making hymns
To the liquor of your laughter
        And the lacquer of your limbs.

But you turn across the table
        A telescope of eyes,
And it lights a Russian sable
        Running circles in the skies . . .

Till I go running after,
        Obeying all your whims—
For the liquor of your laughter
        And the lacquer of your limbs.

Writing the Spectra poems from a place within himself he did not yet
clearly know, he allowed new qualities of person and style to emerge: he

indulged in an open acceptance of sex and liquor and in a flirtation with decadence; he found it easy to commit to direct statements that had an absurd, almost surrealistic juxtaposition of elements; he began to write with an elliptical quality that had similarities to Asian poetry; and he was able to delight in wild and contagious humor. What is modern and original in Bynner's work begins with the Spectra poems and is present, at first, without his awareness, expressed in his rather outrageous attack on the contemporary styles of poetry.

≡

Arthur Davison Ficke, the other writer of the Spectra poems, would remain Bynner's closest friend, his mentor, and a man who acted like a father figure. Genuinely concerned for Bynner's welfare and truly fond of him, Ficke was not homosexual and not involved with Bynner in any way that was threatening to him. A lawyer who largely did not practice, Ficke was a writer of very controlled, intellectual poetry, a novel on Mexico (where he first went with Bynner), and a book on Japanese prints, which he seriously collected. It was Ficke who first took Bynner to Asia and introduced him to Asian culture. Interestingly, neither Bynner nor Ficke particularly admired the other's poetry.

Besides their years together as students, friends, and poets, Bynner and Ficke shared a deep attachment to Edna St. Vincent Millay, and she to them. They discovered her verse in November 1912, just after she published "Renascence," and they immediately wrote her a fan letter; eventually the three met. The relationship among them is fascinating in the ways it operated and in what they seem to have understood, accepted, and encouraged in one another. She was deeply in love with Ficke and wrote some of her most important and passionate sonnets about him, but he never chose to marry her, a subject they must have discussed, as Millay was to remain a close friend of Ficke's and of his two wives. She did accept Bynner's proposal of marriage, but it is likely that neither the proposal nor the acceptance was serious. In identical letters to each, Ficke explained why a marriage was not wise and that if any two of them married, the three could not remain as close. Millay settled in Austerlitz, New York, a small town southeast of Albany near the Massachusetts border. Ficke bought a house in Hillsdale, the town just south of Austerlitz, and moved there with his second wife. Bynner frequently visited them in this area. Millay had married a Dutchman, Eugen Boissevain, whom Bynner and Ficke had first met in 1917 on the boat to China. It is not at all incidental to the complexity of this fascinating *ménage,* one that someday should be fully and thoughtfully explored, that Millay was also a lesbian and later in life addicted to drugs, facts that Ficke, Bynner, and Boissevain knew.

≡≡≡

It was in March 1917 that Bynner went to Japan and China for four months, and he was in China again from June 1920 until April 1921. Between these trips he spent a year or more traveling in the United States. He taught a poetry class at Berkeley; published *Grenstone Poems* (1917) and *The Beloved Stranger* (1919); met a Chinese scholar, Kiang Kang-hu, with whom he began to translate an anthology of three hundred T'ang poems, from the finest period of Chinese poetry; and he experienced his first acknowledged love affair with the Swiss artist Paul Thévenaz. This chaotic series of events took place between his thirty-fifth and fortieth years, although it took him eight more years to finish translating the T'ang poems.

All of this coincided with the First World War. Bynner was deeply against war and, because he refused to fight, lost many friends. He turned to Asia as if to seek some special understanding from a different source. He was to say in later life that during World War I he turned to China and began a translation, and that he did the same in World War II, when he translated Laotzu. Asia represented many things for Bynner, but it was especially an avenue into a way of life that was comforting and compatible to him as a man and a poet.

Grenstone Poems represented his first book as a mature poet, and it shows an advance in his control of diction and less indulgence in sentimental thoughts. Most of the poems were written before Bynner began the Spectra poems. As such, *Grenstone Poems* often lacks the clarity of his later lyrics, but it shows Bynner beginning to master the art of the lyric, the type of poem he so often wrote, and to create a style distinctively his own.

At the Last

There is no denying
That it matters little,
When through a narrow door
We enter a room together,
Which goes after, which before.

Perhaps you are not dying:
Perhaps—there is no knowing—
I shall slip by and turn and laugh with you
Because it mattered so little,
The order of our going.

Driftwood

Come, warm your hands
From the cold wind of time.
I have built here, under the moon,
A many-colored fire
With fragments of wood
That have been part of a tree
And part of a ship.
Were leaves more real,
Or driven nails.
Or fingers of builders,
Than these burning violets?
Come, warm your hands
From the cold wind of time.
There's a fire under the moon.

Richard Wilbur discusses "Driftwood" in his introduction to *The Works of Witter Bynner: Selected Poems*, and in doing so provides an understanding of the quality that exists in Bynner's best lyrics, a quality that can be easily overlooked unless the simple complexity of the lyric is appreciated.

That is a disciplined free-verse poem, varying narrowly between lines of two and three stresses, and disposed in two paragraphs of seven lines each. It is about a fire made of driftwood on a chill, gusty, and moonlit beach, and the poet invites us to share it. The words never forsake their literal subject, and continually render the scene more vivid to the eye: driftwood does in fact burn with many colors, and through the mention of leaves, nails, shipbuilders' fingers, and violets we imagine the several shapes and behaviors of the flames. But of course the cold wind of the second line is not merely a wind: it is also "time." The poet invites us to meditate, in the presence of a driftwood fire, on that time which coldly destroys all things, bringing down the tallest tree and wrecking the best-made vessel. We are asked whether the tree and the ship were "more real" than their now

burning fragments, and it is assumed that we know the answer. . . .
The fire, as Bynner describes it, is not simply the annihilation of
wood fragments; even as the wrecked ship of the poem was built of
felled trees, the fire is something "built" of ship's driftwood by the
poet's hands and offered us as a warming symbolic proof that time
is not a destroyer but a perpetual renewer. Out of all change comes
new life, as in the variously colored violets of spring; we are to warm
our hands at flames in which we see the fingers of dead builders, and
then turn to fresh work; and the moon, above such a fire, is a light
which forever rises and waxes again.

This brief, plain-seeming, subtle poem, in which all the words
prove to be working hard, and in which the meaning seems to
emerge uncoerced from the data . . . points toward the best qualities
of Bynner's later achievements.

Unfortunately, Bynner did not often reach this level of achievement,
in which the lyric is a finely observed experience in a strong but simple
language. So fluent and at ease, so much a poet of occasion, he too often
published work that was not substantial.

The T'ang poems that Bynner began at this time were translated from
the literal texts of Dr. Kiang Kang-hu, a member of a distinguished Chinese family, a noted scholar, and a social activist who had been forced to
leave China because of his liberal views. Bynner and Kiang had met in
Berkeley, where each was teaching and where Kiang had left a portion of
his large collection of Chinese manuscripts. They worked together there
and in China, and most often by mail. The anthology has always been
popular and is a considerable achievement in its accurate and sensitive
rendering of poems thought of as Chinese classics and very difficult to
translate. The concise and realistic quality of these poems, especially the
shih poems, usually of eight lines, is often perfectly captured by Bynner
and Kiang. Burton Watson describes the character of these poems in *The
Works of Witter Bynner: The Chinese Translations* and illustrates the qualities in these poems that Bynner so admired and would emulate more and
more as he continued to write.

If his [the poet's] mood is one of melancholy or apprehension, as
is usually the case in T'ang poetry, he will customarily relate the
emotion to a particular event in his life—parting from a friend, frustration in his career, the loneliness of a journey, or the pain of exile.
His poem of grief will typically be given up almost entirely to a de-
piction of the scene of his sorrowing, the physical surroundings at
the time he experiences the emotion, presenting what we now term

objective correlatives of his inner state. And in the closing lines, when he comes to describe the emotion itself, he almost never seeks to analyze or philosophize upon it, much less exploit it for display of individualism. Instead his statement is deliberately couched in language that is conventionalized, self-effacing, and low-keyed, ending the poem on a note that will often strike the present-day reader as anticlimactic.

Not only the poems but China itself deeply influenced Bynner. His two trips there involved extensive travel throughout the country, unusual for an American. Bynner often traveled with and as a "native." He collected scrolls and jades on both trips, later wrote extensively on China for periodicals at a time when China was not well understood, and brought not only the style of T'ang poets but their point of view into his poetry. Bynner found in the statement of a Chinese scholar, Ku Hung-ming, a concept he often quoted that is important and appropriate to himself: "The real Chinaman is a man who lives the life of a man of adult reason with the heart of a child: the head of a grown-up man and the heart of a child. The Chinese spirit, therefore, is a spirit of perpetual youth." While much in Bynner's character can be exasperating, it is better understood and perhaps more appreciated if seen in this way, which embodies the inconsistency Bynner so relished throughout his life.

What Bynner and Kiang achieved in their translations can be illustrated by their versions of poems by one of the greatest T'ang poets, Li Po, a man addicted to wine and yet revered as a supreme master of Chinese poetic sensibility, and a poet Bynner intensely admired. These poems are typical of Li Po's work, of the *shih* style, and of the kind of Chinese poem Bynner found so fitting to his own sensibility as a poet.

Drinking Alone with the Moon

From a pot of wine among the flowers
I drank alone. There was no one with me—
Till raising my cup, I asked the bright moon
To bring me my shadow and make us three.
Alas, the moon was unable to drink
And my shadow tagged me vacantly;
But still for a while I had these friends
To cheer me through the end of spring. . . .
I sang. The moon encouraged me.
I danced. My shadow tumbled after.
As long as I knew, we were boon companions

And then I was drunk, and we lost one another.
. . . Shall goodwill ever be secure?
I watched the long road of the River of Stars.

A Farewell to a Friend

With a blue line of mountains north of the wall,
And east of the city a white curve of water,
Here you must leave me and drift away
Like a loosened water-plant hundreds of miles. . . .
I shall think of you in a floating cloud;
So in the sunset think of me.
. . . We wave our hands to say good-bye,
And my horse is neighing again and again.

Richard Wilbur discusses this last poem as illustrating Bynner's qualities as a fine translator, as showing what Bynner admired in Chinese poetry of the T'ang period, and as indicating what he brought into his own poetry from the Chinese.

This exemplary translation illustrates everything which Bynner found attractive and corrective in Chinese poetry. Everything is distributed, in these quiet lines, with an evenness of attention; there is nothing of what Yeats called "insubordination of detail," and there are no ostentatious felicities of language. Everything in the scene and situation is actual, and presented in a natural sequence. The figures of speech involve no violent amalgamations: that is, if one's friend is going on a river journey, it is reasonable to think of a loosened water plant; that done, since the poem occurs under the open sky, it is not hard to associate the traveler with a floating cloud as well, and the poet's sinking heart with the sunset. The horse in the last line is neighing for equine reasons, but I suspect that we are to be reminded of the sounds of human grief.

The poems in *The Beloved Stranger,* Bynner's next book, written after the Spectra poems and largely after beginning the Chinese translation, are far superior to most of his earlier work. They combine the fine lyric voice and simple diction, the sharp edge of the Spectra poems, and the discipline he was taking from his translation work. For the first time, Bynner spoke in his distinctive voice and his work began to express the elements that are so often found in his best poems: the unexpected observation, the wit, the sharply observed but often ordinary situation expressed in a brief line and a short poem, the sense of the surreal or of the reality beyond the immediate, and the ordinary, almost flat language and syntax. The best poetry Bynner would write seems to bring together the lyric and Spectra styles *and* move toward the commonplace situations and the style that are found in the brief T'ang poems.

The Wall

How is it,
That you, whom I can never know,
My beloved,
Are a wall between me and those I have known well—
So that my familiars vanish
Farther than the blue roofs of Nankow
And are lost among the desert hills?

Lightning

There is a solitude in seeing you,
Followed by your presence when you are gone.
You are like heaven's veins of lightning.
I cannot see till afterward
How beautiful you are.
There is blindness in seeing you,
Followed by the sight of you when you are gone.

≡

Something must be said about Paul Thévenaz and about the University of California at Berkeley, for both were significant experiences in Bynner's life during this time. It is clear that the experience with Thévenaz represented something important to Bynner and to his poetry. Thévenaz was not Bynner's first homosexual lover, nor his first serious one, but theirs was the relationship that up to this time most affected Bynner. Thévenaz's name is now generally unknown, yet he once worked in Paris with Cocteau and Stravinsky, painting portraits of them, of the Countess de Noailles, and of others; he also designed interiors of several New York houses and had exhibitions at Knoedler's in 1917 and the Chicago Arts Club in 1921, just before his death at thirty-one. He is a figure in several of Florine Stettheimer's multicharacter portraits of creative life in New York City. There, with Thévenaz, are Marcel Duchamp, Carl Van Vechten and his wife, Fania Marinoff, the photographer Arnold Genthe, and the sculptor Elie Nadelman.
Bynner's eulogy of Thévenaz, in prose and poetry, was published in

the *New York Times* just after Thévenaz's death in July 1921 of a ruptured appendix. From this man, Bynner learned to accept openly his emotional nature and to enjoy life with ease and lightness. Thévenaz was no more "serious" than Florine Stettheimer and her art were, but each suggests something important about the time and the period and about an approach to life and art. Their art touches upon an aspect of our existence that is childlike and delightful but still potent in its youthful and romantic abandon to friendship and a form of spontaneous creativity. Such art is naïve and "light," but if one ignores it, one misses a significant human and creative expression. Thévenaz said: "If one has personality, it will come through, no matter what one does"; the expression of personality was as important to him as to Bynner. One of Bynner's poems to Thévenaz, published in *Caravan* (1925), contains lines that suggest the painter's unusual qualities:

> Tradition he would set at naught,
> And never shed a tear:
> No scripture we were ever taught
> Accords with his career.
>
> Persons who conserve the race
> With families and fatigue
> He would encounter face to face
> And never care a fig.
>
> He would snap his fingers at the young
> And thumb his nose at the old,
> Believing in some of the things that are sung
> But in none of the things that are told . . .

Probably it was Thévenaz's light-hearted, youthful directness, his open acceptance of himself and others, that appealed to Bynner, providing him with a model of artistic and personal expression as individual and strong as the New England expression of his own family and as contagiously free as the spirit of his Spectra poems. Like the Spectra poems, the experience with Thévenaz was a deeply personal release that affected Bynner and his poetry. The briefness of the relationship, and the loss, would also affect Bynner's sense of the transitory quality of life. In a very serious way the relationship with Thévenaz confirmed Bynner's fear that he must always keep a protective distance between himself and anyone he loved.

When he went to California, Bynner was most attracted to Berkeley and the Bay area and decided early in his stay to make it his home. He was there to do "military service"; he had been hired to teach public speaking to the Students Auxiliary Training Corps at the university. When the war ended a month after he arrived in 1918, he was asked to teach verse writing the next term. About twenty students were officially in the class, but many others came. There were no texts or tests; poems were read and criticized; often there were guests—Ficke, John Cowper Powys, Stella Benson; and often the class met outdoors. He celebrated Whitman's centennial with his class in an outdoor reading of *Leaves of Grass* by Powys, Charles Erskine Scott Wood, himself, and others. For its time the class was highly unconventional, and it was vividly remembered by the students. They gave him a dinner for eighty people and published in his honor a book of their verse called *W. B. in California*. Bynner's class included and helped to develop several poets and literary figures of the California School: Genevieve Taggard, Eda Lou Walton, Hildegarde Flanner, Idella Purnell Stone, Ernest Walsh, David Greenhood, and Stanton A. Coblentz.

Bynner also participated energetically in the social life of the Bay area's literary figures: he knew the writers Jack London and George Sterling; Bruce Porter, the painter and designer who married William James's daughter; John Henry Nash and Porter Garnett, both excellent fine art printers; Beniamino Bufano, the sculptor, who went to China with Bynner in 1920; and Albert M. Bender, an extraordinary Irish Jew who supported the arts by means of his successful insurance business. Bynner was in the Bohemian Club and was about to write the 1920 Grove play for this men's group when he was caught in a bitter controversy over his support of the release of conscientious objectors from prison. Bynner was threatened by civic leaders and the issue was in all the papers. Bynner was also accused of drinking too much at a Mardi Gras ball and of serving liquor to freshmen in his rooms—both of which he admitted to the university authorities to be true, and to be incorrect behavior for a professor. Compelled to return east to see his stepsister just before her death, Bynner abandoned the play and the city that he had once seen as his new home.

≡

After returning from his second visit to China in 1921, Bynner went to New York, but he soon decided, once again, that he must get away from home or at least leave his mother and New York. With low spirits and low energy, Bynner began, in January 1922, another lecture tour. It was almost as if these trips had become a search for a place he could remain. He had some belongings in his mother's apartment in the Hotel Seymour on West 45th Street; others in the Homer Saint-Gaudens house in Cornish; some of his Chinese scrolls, jades, and wood carvings in a friend's house in Berkeley; and all his other possessions in his hotel rooms at the Hotel Carlton on the corner of Telegraph and Durant in Berkeley. He and his possessions were literally dispersed across the country, and he was, at forty-one, tired of wandering.

His lecture tour took him through the Southwest, and on his way there he went to the University of Oklahoma where he met and advised Lynn Riggs, a young student who later followed Bynner to New Mexico, became his lover, and served briefly as his secretary. Riggs was the future writer of the play *Green Grow the Lilacs,* from which Oscar Hammerstein II and Richard Rodgers adapted *Oklahoma.* Bynner traveled on, exhausted from a heavy cold that would not leave him. In this poor condition he arrived in Santa Fe, New Mexico, on February 20, 1922. Except for brief vacations and extended trips to a second house in Chapala, Mexico, this town and the first house he occupied in it, at 342 Buena Vista Street, would remain his home until he died on June 1, 1968.

Bynner went to Santa Fe to see a friend, the painter Willard Nash, and at the invitation of Alice Corbin Henderson. Mrs. Henderson had helped Harriet Monroe found *Poetry* magazine in Chicago in 1912, and she had been continuing her editorial work from Santa Fe, where she had come in 1916 to be cured of tuberculosis. She was the center of the writing community in Santa Fe, and through her husband, William Penhallow Henderson, the painter, architect, and furniture designer, was also greatly involved in the painting scene. Santa Fe and a neighboring town, Taos, seventy miles north, had begun to attract American painters— Robert Henri, John Sloan, Edward Hopper, John Marin, Marsden Hartley, George Bellows, Andrew Dasburg, and, later, Georgia O'Keeffe and others.

Santa Fe was small, just over seven thousand people. Those who spoke only English were a minority among the Spanish-speaking people who had first explored the area in the 1540s and settled Santa Fe in 1610, ten years before the Pilgrims arrived at Plymouth. The light was brilliant, the air was clear, the long views of the desert and mountains often suggested some land not American. Bynner said (as others have) that the terrain is like Peking's, as are the houses enclosed in courtyards of adobe walls, and that the Indians are like the Chinese in manner and character. Both north and south of Santa Fe are the 800-to-1,000-year-old settlements of the Pueblo Indians, their adobe buildings rising in the air like the mountains behind them. In 1922, the streets of Santa Fe were unpaved. Automobiles were few and donkeys loaded with piñon wood a common sight. Indian, Spanish, and Anglo-American cultures were reflected in the architecture, and you could see members of all three groups daily in the streets of the town. It was a place that seemed to many Anglos, as it seemed to Bynner, exotic and even unique. It was a place of great history and culture, a place as tolerant and as different to an American as Paris, and some artists spoke of it this way. Two years after his arrival Bynner described Santa Fe:

> On Sunday evenings when the band played, youths would stream in one direction round the Plaza and in the opposite direction maidens, just as apart from one another and just as aware of one another as I have seen them in Mexican cities. Older women moved nunlike, on Sundays or weekdays, with soft black shawls over their heads, the fringe hanging down their dresses. Burros came daily in droves with round burdens of firewood, or with riders from the country whose heels bumped lazily from a jiggling trot. Though there was no longer an open market in the Plaza, there was one street left where wagons, from ranches or from Indian villages, held corn, tomatoes, apples, melons and other fresh produce to be bought directly from dark-eyed drivers. On the roads radiating from town were many views and few signboards. In doorways, on street-corners, were many groups speaking Spanish and few speaking English. In the Legislature were interpreters nimbly moving from one member to another and nimbly re-phrasing remarks into English or Spanish On the outlying hills were venturous artists in sombreros, corduroys and bright neckerchiefs. When Holy Days came, there were bonfires and the Virgin or St. Francis was carried through the streets by walking worshippers. And round about the landscape, in their snug, earthen pueblos, were Indians, guarding the dignity of their race and instinctively living the beauty of their religion and their art, as they had been doing for hundreds of years.

The main hotel had burned the month before he arrived, so Bynner stayed at the tuberculosis sanatorium, Sunmount He himself was not well and after a few days canceled his speaking tour in order to rest in a town that had greeted him and his lecture, "The Heart of China," with great enthusiasm. There were many teas and parties lasting long past midnight, and he would walk home with a lantern along the Camino del Monte Sol just as the sun came over the Sangre de Cristo mountains and spread across the still, black desert.

After only a few weeks Bynner made the decision to stay in Santa Fe. He was able to rent a small adobe house from the artist Paul Burlin. He then went to Berkeley briefly, via the Grand Canyon, but returned in June to remain indefinitely, he said. The town was a comfortable place for a writer. Alice Corbin had brought other writers to Santa Fe to speak:

Vachel Lindsay and Carl Sandburg, both friends of Bynner's, lectured there shortly before and after he did. Many others had come for extended visits, like Glenway Wescott and Yvor Winters; and many more would come to visit briefly, like Robert Frost, Arthur Ficke, Edna Millay, Thornton Wilder, W. H. Auden, Stephen Spender, and Aldous Huxley. It seemed that, in time, everyone passed through Santa Fe, en route to the West Coast, or returning to the East. Removed from the East and its pressures, Bynner enjoyed living in a community where the artist and writer mattered, where there was a tradition of individual action in varied cultural patterns, and where the cultures were part of a living historical continuity. The city was gossipy, but so was he, and it tolerated what it talked about, recognizing that in a land as ancient as this, little was new or impossible. This provocative place seemed to fit his sense of America and his sense of himself.

≡≡≡

In Taos, where Bynner went for a long visit in July, lived Mabel Dodge Sterne. Known as a great patron of the arts in Europe and in New York, and as an "advanced" woman, an experimenter with life, and a collector of people, she had come to New Mexico in 1917 a jaded Easterner and found in the sun and land, and especially in the Indians, a source for renewal. She divorced her painter husband, Maurice Sterne, began to build an elaborate house, and in 1923 married an Indian, Tony Luhan. She brought people to New Mexico and to Taos—famous people. She wanted to inspire the great. Bynner, whom she had met in New York, was summoned to Taos and came. At first the spectacle of the vast desert landscape at Taos, the curve of the mountains behind it, the pueblo, and Mabel's generosity pleased him, but it soon became apparent that they were not easy companions. She wanted to dominate everyone, and Bynner was not someone who easily let anyone control his life.

Their first ostensible problem had to do with Bynner's secretary, Willard Johnson, called "Spud." A student at Berkeley, founder there of *Laughing Horse,* a clever satirical publication that went with him when he came to live with Bynner, Johnson was a quiet, subtle wit, slight and shy, and, finally, rather lazy about his talent. As he grew older he looked like a monk, and his single, quiet life became almost monastic. Bynner and he were lovers, but Spud was too indecisive to satisfy Bynner for long—he didn't respond to Bynner's teaching with alacrity. Mabel gradually won over Spud and eventually took him to Taos to become her own secretary. The current of this incident ran below the surface from the start.

The real issue between them concerned the D. H. Lawrences, whom

Mabel had invited to visit her. It all began in September 1922, when Mabel arrived at Bynner's adobe house in Santa Fe saying it was too late in the day to drive her guests to Taos. She asked Bynner if he would let the Lawrences spend the night. They were tired and uncertain about New Mexico and Mabel, and Lawrence was especially belligerent about a painted board from a wooden Sicilian cart that Tony had accidentally cracked. Bynner's laughter, Spud's quiet humor, plus the evident good will of everyone relaxed the tensions that night. The next morning, William Penhallow Henderson and his daughter, "Little Alice," who was later to marry Mabel's only son, John Evans, came over to make the breakfast. The car finally went off. In it: Mabel in command; Tony, the silent Indian, driving; and the Lawrences, one full of open response, the other so aggressively and eagerly waiting to be convinced, both beginning another journey in their endless search to find a place in which he could live. It is worth noting about these restless spirits that Lawrence was 37, Bynner 41, Frieda 43, and Mabel 43 when they met in Santa Fe in 1922.

Bynner and the Lawrences met again, and early in 1923 a message came from Lawrence asking Bynner and Spud to go to Mexico with them in March. They all met in Mexico City, and from there they traveled throughout the country. It was a strange journey, tense with emotions that generated some of Lawrence's best essays and his novel *The Plumed Serpent*, in which Bynner is a minor character. It also resulted in Bynner's best volume of poems, *Indian Earth* (1929); three fine portraits of Lawrence in verse, "D. H. Lawrence," "Lorenzo," and "A Foreigner"; and the book of the trip that Bynner published in 1951, *Journey with Genius: Recollections and Reflections concerning the D. H. Lawrences.*

The relationships were unusual. Bynner and Spud were lovers and friends, but also father and son, teacher and student. Perhaps Lawrence wanted to be all of these to each, or at least some of them. He was fascinated by Bynner's energetic assurance, which insisted on seeing the light and the pleasant where Lawrence saw the dark and the difficult. He felt, correctly, that Bynner avoided issues, but Lawrence could not openly admit—although he no doubt knew—that he himself did not always face the truth. They wrestled in their minds for a victory, but in such a contest there is no winner. Frieda loved her husband, but she also enjoyed Bynner; after Lawrence's death she returned to Taos and remained close friends with Bynner. Spud refused to commit himself to anyone, which did not bother Frieda but slightly disturbed both his teachers—it was an affront to their doctrines.

What went on was the unspoken contest of wills that often exists in life and that was so much a part of the fiction Lawrence wrote. He and

Bynner existed somewhere between Gerald and Birkin in *Women in Love* and the Captain and his peasant orderly in Lawrence's story "The Prussian Officer." It was a relationship that could not be resolved because it could not admit the full possibility of love between men, nor could it admit the equality of such love. If Lawrence saw Bynner as too gregarious, as hiding a fear of intimacy in a light-hearted manner, Bynner saw Lawrence as a man equally afraid of intimacy, as hiding behind his severe criticism of Frieda and much of the world he met. The intensity of what Lawrence and Bynner felt was very great, too great to allow them to relax together. Each had been understood and challenged in a dimension that was deep and important.

Journey with Genius describes the relationship. It shows each as he was, Bynner no better than Lawrence. To Lawrence's ardent followers, Bynner's account is incorrect and irreverent, but others can see that it is Bynner's journey with a genius who was also a deeply flawed man suffering from severe illness. It was one of the first books that revealed the complex Lawrence personality that has emerged in more recent years: brilliant, sensitive, stubborn, angry, and repressed. Lawrence wrote Bynner fine letters, full of genuine affection and good will, and praised Bynner's book of verse containing the long, critical poem about Lawrence as "very sincere and really deep in life. Even serving happiness is no joke." Bynner returned to Chapala, the town that Lawrence had found in Mexico, and said of it that "no place on earth has given me so much at once." He returned year after year and finally bought the house in which he wrote his Lawrence memoir. He never lost Lawrence. It seems that in each man there was a self that attracted and repelled, irrevocably and inexplicably. Bynner's poem "Lorenzo" comes as close to defining this conflict as he was able to:

> I had not known that there could be
> Men like Lorenzo and like me,
> Both in the world and both so right
> That the world is dark and the world is light.
> I had not thought that anyone
> Would choose the dark for dwelling on,
> Would dig and delve for the bitterest roots
> Of sweetest and suavest fruits.
> I never had presumed to doubt
> That now and then the light went out;
> But I had not known that there could be
> Men like Lorenzo and like me
> Both in the world and both so right

That the world is dark and the world is light.
I had not guessed that joy could be
Selected for an enemy.

Mabel's possessive nature never forgave Bynner for going with Law-rence and for the affection Frieda felt for him, and she sought revenge by taking Spud and by accusing Bynner, later in life, of having brought homosexuality to New Mexico—an accusation so imaginative and wild in its vindictiveness as to be almost forgivable. Bynner had his own re-venge—for it must be said that neither was a creature without venom. In 1926 he wrote a play about Mabel, née Ganson, then Evans, Dodge, Sterne, and Luhan, and called it *Cake.* It is about a woman jaded by life who seeks relief from her boredom in travel, drink, sex, religion, death, and finally in cake. It is a verse play, elaborately stylized, a spoof that has many brilliant qualities; today we would call it high camp. The play por-trays modern woman as emasculator, goddess of wealth, and deceiver of both men and herself, but very much her own mistress/master. It is witty and nasty fun that in its style and tone, as well as its subject matter, is quite ahead of its time. The Lady in *Cake,* for all her faults, is seen by Bynner as a liberated woman, free to discover her character and her place in the world; the play is principally an attack on the materialism and de-structiveness of American society and not on the American female. Here is a brief passage from the opening scene of the play that illustrates the style and tone:

THE LADY

The trouble with me is I'm bored with being bored.
How long this living takes! How long, O Lord!
I have had seven husbands—and that's enough, I think.
I have come through mysticism, free love, and drink.
I am offered everything money can buy,
And yet there's nothing I want—not even to die.

THE UNICORN

(With a blow on the gong)
The smelling salts!

THE LADY

    (Restraining one of the SERVANTS, with an indifferently raised
    hand)
I am Victorian,
To be given a sniff of tears by any man?
The world has moved, since women kept their hearts
As sticky as a dish of apple tarts.
It's different now: I know what I'm about;
I am a modernist. I am tired out.
I must find me a chamberlain who understands!

THE UNICORN

    (Hastily)
Shall it be psycho-analysis?—or glands?

THE LADY

Order me everything that you can think of.
There isn't a liquor left I want a drink of.
Order me anything. I'm desperate!

THE UNICORN

There's a famous doctor below. I had him wait.
What ho! Bring on the Psychoanalyst!
    (He strikes the gong. Four additional SERVANTS bring into the
    Presence the PSYCHOANALYST, a tiny man with not enough
    beard to conceal his thin neck.)

THE PSYCHOANALYST

    (Going straight to the LADY)
Yes, I can see at once that you resist.

THE LADY

I don't.

THE PSYCHOANALYST

You've proved it. Let me feel your dream!
(Feeling her pulse)
Your need of psychospection is extreme.
Turn over on the other dream a minute.

It is not necessary to burden *Cake* with too much critical apparatus, but it has aspects that are worth noting beyond its relationship to Mabel Luhan, its relationship to the modern woman, and its style of high camp so advanced for its time. William Jay Smith, in his introduction to *The Works of Witter Bynner: Light Verse and Satires,* analyzes the play itself and says that it "reads like an amalgam of Noel Coward, Cole Porter and Ionesco, with echoes of Oscar Wilde." He believes that "it may be a mistake to claim too much for the symbolism of *Cake,* which so clearly makes fun of itself, but the play has a remarkably resonant depth that may be lost sight of because of its brilliant surface."

He then suggests some parallels to the plays of T. S. Eliot. Smith notes that *Cake* was finished in June 1926 and published that fall, just as Eliot published the first part of *Sweeney Agonistes* in the *New Criterion;* the second part was published in January 1927. Smith says: "In both [*Cake* and *Sweeney Agonistes*], the action is stylized as in Noh drama and the characters are caricatures, bent on having a 'good time.' Both make use of vaudeville routines and catch in their dialogue the syncopated beat of jazz." He refers to other parallels and then says:

When Eliot wrote *The Cocktail Party* twenty years after *Sweeney Agonistes,* he drew on his earlier play and may also have had a look at *Cake. The Cocktail Party* opens with an inane cocktail conversation in which Celia asks Julia to tell the story "about Lady Klootz and the wedding cake." The story about Lady Klootz, who according to Julia, "had too much vitality," never gets told, but "cake" and "gin" become the key words in the first scene. Food and drink take on symbolic significance in both plays: in *The Cocktail Party* there is the mess concocted for Edward in the kitchen using up all the eggs, and in *Cake* all the references to cake with their many obvious implications. In both plays, cocktail libations are offered up at the turning point of the action. Both plays mock the modern fetish of psychiatry. Sir Henry Harcourt-Reilly, the psychiatrist, admonishes the characters in *The Cocktail Party* in the words of the dying Buddha to his disciples: "Work out your salvation with diligence"; and the Mandarin in *Cake* (the Asian doctor), invoking Laotzu, advises the Lady:

"Lean with the wind. Accept the universe." Both plays make pointed use of the black humor of cannibalism, and I dare say that *Cake* and *The Cocktail Party* are the only two modern verse dramas—or dramas of any sort for that matter—in which a society woman meets her death in a remote place beside an anthill. I do not wish to belabor the possibility that *Cake* is yet another source for *The Cocktail Party* (the plays are totally different in tone), but only to suggest that *Cake* is a highly entertaining and original comedy that deserves far more attention than it has received.

≡≡≡

Most of the events in Bynner's early Santa Fe life were not so dramatic. The years were divided into many months in Santa Fe, a few in Chapala, and one or two in New York visiting his mother and brother and friends. These visits continued to upset him and he clearly saw that he preferred to remain in Santa Fe. The adobe shack he lived in was bought and added to, Chinese scrolls and gold-painted woodwork installed, Indian blankets used as thick curtains and on chairs, and Hispanic santos placed throughout the house. Over the years the simple three-room shack grew to a large, complicated, eccentric house surrounded by high trees and hedges. The house in details of architecture was at once Indian, Hispanic, and Chinese, and in time became a reflection of Bynner's character as it rambled, changed shape and style, opened up and closed inward, with its different textures, various colors, and many dark tones.

He entered into the community: into its politics, running once for the state legislature—as a Democrat—and losing; into the preservation of its old and varied past; into its great September Fiesta, which he saw as an occasion for wild fun and during which, for many years, he led the parade in some costume, all six foot two of him, with Dolly Sloan—John Sloan's wife—as his tiny, less-than-five-foot partner; into its poetry readings and discussions, its community theater, its art exhibits; and of course into its social life. The last could occupy so much time in Santa Fe that Bynner established the rule, written on a sign for him by John Sloan, that no one should call at his house before five in the evening. Then began drinks, dinner, and card games or talk until any hour of the morning. After the guests left, he wrote, going to bed at dawn. He would rise at one, have breakfast, answer letters, which he did with great care, and write again or garden until it was five.

No one minded waiting for him until that hour, for when Witter Bynner came into a group, it was brought alive in a way that to most people seemed delightful and personal, as if this were a special occasion meant only for them. He told stories, made endless puns, drank and smoked constantly, did monologues, played old tunes on the piano, imitated his mother in her usual role of demanding more attention, or a toothless old aunt in some endless family narrative, recited limericks or poetry in a voice that even in old recordings is strong, mellow, and cultivated. With his head, now quite bald, and his large, strong body always browned by gardening in the sun; his clothes often individual—a velvet Navajo blouse in dark blue, a large turquoise-and-silver belt, and wide white pants or one of his beautifully embroidered Chinese robes with great sleeves; his gestures and movements strong, quick, affirmative, as was his walk; his laugh that would soar high above the noise of a room like the whoop of a crane—he was a vibrant figure in the landscape of Santa Fe.

≡≡≡

When he first came to Santa Fe, he had successively several male secretaries who ran the house for him, typed his letters and poems, and carried out administrative details. They were, in several instances, also his lovers. He worked in the garden but never bothered with household matters. The cooking and cleaning were left to Rita Fadilla, a Spanish-speaking neighbor on College Street (or the Old Santa Fe Trail, as it is now called) who came to Bynner soon after he arrived in Santa Fe and stayed until her death in 1963, some forty years later. She was the majordomo and Bynner her *patrón* whom she served devotedly and protectively; in turn, he fed her family from his kitchen, a family that always seemed to be growing, and saw to it that she and they were provided for. She was a wiry, dark-skinned, dark-haired woman, full of superstitions, to whom some attributed special powers, but she was mostly just a proud woman who served Bynner with a passionate love that never changed and that seemed to others so excessive that they explained it as diabolical. Rita remained a single constant in Bynner's life. She expressed her character in this letter she wrote him:

Maybe you think that when you go away nobody remember you. But I do specially when you're sick. You know me. You know that I rather for you to put tears for me than me for you. Last night I feel so bad for you that I cry lots, and little Celia asked what wrong with me and I say "my feet." I wish I am a little bird that I can stay with you in the day and fly to the house to take care of the house at night.

≡≡≡

Alfred A. Knopf had become Bynner's publisher with the appearance of *The Beloved Stranger* in 1919. In 1920 there was a volume of poems, *A Canticle of Pan,* and also *Pins for Wings,* a brief book of short quips that describe other writers, a book Bynner published under the name Emanuel Morgan with Sunwise Turn, Inc. In it T. S. Eliot is described as the "wedding cake / of two tired cultures," and William Carlos Williams as "carbolic acid / in love." *A Book of Plays* appeared in 1922; a translation from the French of Charles Vildrac, *A Book of Love,* in 1923; a volume of verse, *Caravan,* in 1925; then *Cake* in 1926; and *Indian Earth* in 1929, poems about Chapala with a section on the New Mexican Indians. *The Persistence of Poetry,* an essay on verse, was published in San Francisco as a special volume for the Book Club of California and as his introduction to *The Jade Mountain* (1929), his translation from the Chinese that after eleven years finally appeared.

Both *A Canticle of Pan* and *Caravan* continued Bynner's new strong voice, but they also included some of the weaker lyrics that Bynner had so easily written before Spectra and the Chinese translations. *Caravan* contains "Epithalamium and Elegy," one of Bynner's finest lyric poems, and it includes the first of his three poems on Lawrence. It is *Indian Earth,* the next book, that is Bynner's best single volume up to this time, and perhaps his best book. Bynner dedicated it to D. H. Lawrence. It is the one that balances the lyric quality with other interests and introduces an important new subject matter that clearly engages Bynner's democratic spirit: the Pueblo Indians of New Mexico and the Indians of Chapala where he went in Mexico, a small village on a lake of the same name, a little south of Guadalajara.

One Pueblo Indian poem had appeared in *Caravan,* "A Dance for Rain," but in *Indian Earth* there is a series of poems that constitute a section on the Native American of this part of New Mexico. It is fair to say that collectively they represent some of the best poetry to address this aspect of American culture and as such deserve to be far better known. The poems are deeply sympathetic to and knowledgeable about the Pueblo Indians without being sentimental or esoteric. They capture the character and the spirit of the Indians through their religion and their dances, and they contain a feeling for the landscape, the sky, and the elements of nature, such as rain, sun, and wind, that is very much in the spirit of the Pueblo Indians. The poems are written in a language and style that could be described as classic American.

The poems on Chapala are equally fine. Mostly written as eight-line *shih* poems, Bynner makes many Asian references as he sees a relationship between the people of Chapala and the Chinese. Although the poems have a lyric tone, they are not focused on the self and its situation in life but look out at the world of Chapala and especially its native people, whom he sees as possessing a natural dignity and wisdom. Bynner is able to convey this in a clear style and language, and almost completely without self-consciousness.

A Countryman

Swinging a blanket over his left shoulder,
Wearing its bright-colored heart upon his sleeve,
He takes up his bed and walks. It serves him well
For warmth at night on his mat, or in the evening
Against a wind that pours along the lake.
Even at noon it hangs from his neck to his ankle,
Unneeded in the sun except as a king
Always has need to be wearing majesty.

A Beautiful Mexican

There where she sips her wine, her copper brow
Is itself the sunset. Now she has lifted her eyes,
And they are evening stars. I have seen many
Mexican sunsets—but never before had I seen one
Come down from the mountain to be a beautiful woman,
To shadow a table with a dusk of light
From a bare arm and then, alas, to rise
And turn and go, leaving a sudden darkness.

It seemed as though he had found his own voice in these poems, and certainly he was never better known, but the next year, 1930, he described as one of long and lonely depression. He was forty-nine, no longer young, and very much alone. He must have seen that the poetry of his friends Ezra Pound and Wallace Stevens, and of T. S. Eliot, was taking over and that his lyric style was losing ground. Their work was often historical and intellectual in content, engaged with the problems of modern life, generally although not always lacking in the pure lyric quality and in humor, and usually not written in an easily accessible style. Their work was all that Bynner's was not, and he recognized this in his essay *The Persistence of Poetry,* which is, essentially, a justification for his own poetic style: "There are countless artificers, over-cultured and jaded, who with extensive knowledge of the world's poets and with the most highly self-conscious uses of prosody, fabricate words into strained and intellectualized meanings which pass for a season among the literary fashionables as poetry, but which are about as important to the singing heart of man as the latest sartorial trick from Paris."

This harsh outburst is preceded by a statement in which Bynner defines what poetic quality means to him. If poetry is, as he says in this essay, "passionate patience," the best of poetry is for Bynner something quite different from what is usually defined. Bynner remained true to his definition and failed as a poet only when he doubted what he believed, or when he wrote too facilely.

> This passionate gift is genius. And in whatever time it happens, whether it be the time of Li Po or of Homer, of Chaucer or of Shakespeare, it is the rhythm by which men feel their own impulses, their own emotions, their own thoughts. A poet's office is to catch this rhythm and give it to the multitude which has tried to express itself in heart-felt words but has missed the soul-felt rhythm. When a master lives who can so use language that a whole vast sky of words seems as simple as a petal, then the genius arrives who in poetry expresses men to themselves.

Eden Tree, which appeared in 1931, is his version of the modern poem of anxiety, as if in answer to Pound and Eliot, and may well be Bynner's least successful work. An autobiographical sequel to *An Ode to Harvard* and *The New World,* the poem is mostly interesting because it acknowledges Bynner's chaotic and difficult life and addresses his homosexuality. The narrative of the poem is complicated, but it roughly covers events in Bynner's life. He is portrayed as Adam, with references to the good Eve, the lustful Lilith, his muse Celia, and his lover Paul (Thévenaz), and it includes encounters with Christ, Confucius, and Buddha as Adam travels from New York to China. The intention of the poem is explained by Richard Wilbur: "The hope of escaping isolation through universal love is now set aside, and what the poem amounts to is a solitary soul's rehearsal of its wavering progress toward an acceptance of aloneness and self-dependency." While it is a poem that might now be of great interest as issues of homosexuality are more seriously considered, it is not a convincing work. For all its honesty, it is marred by a confusion of incidents and an inability to deal with the hero's anxiety with any intellectual awareness, or to do so in a style that commands belief. It very much lacks the qualities Bynner did not admire in modern poetry, the qualities that distinguish Pound and Eliot. It demonstrates dramatically that Bynner could not write the kind of poem he claimed not to respect.

It was with his personal and poetic world very much in confusion, and while he was writing *Eden Tree,* that Robert Nicholas Montague Hunt came to visit him. Bynner had met Hunt in 1924 through the novelist and historian Paul Horgan, and had seen Hunt briefly again in Santa Fe in 1926 and in Los Angeles for a production of *Cake* in 1928. Hunt came in 1930 only for a visit to recuperate from an illness, but he remained with Bynner until 1964, when he died. Bynner was to turn fifty on August 10, 1931. At the start of the relationship, in November 1930, Bynner wrote to Arthur Ficke and to Albert Bender, his friend in San Francisco. The letters reveal in the phrasing the evident pleasure that bubbles through the correct exterior.

> You will be interested to know that Bobby Hurt suddenly descended on me ten days ago. He encountered someone who had a return ticket from California, expiring on October 31st. He seized it on the eve of its expiration and landed here to my great delight. He had been working twelve to fourteen hours a day for six months, as Assistant Manager and Treasurer of the Paramount Public Theatres in Portland, Oregon, had broken down under the strain and was convalescing in Palo Alto when this chance came to come to Santa Fe. It is extremely pleasant for me to have him here. . . . The vague depression that has held me, more or less, all summer, has now entirely lifted.

> Bobby Hurt suddenly jumped to Santa Fe. . . . He is a delightful fellow. Beginning with poetic fumblings, he has come through entirely on his own efforts to an ability to write down clear-cut and beautiful verse. He wants to stay here, as he puts it "forever." I am trying to find him a job.

Bob, Bobby sometimes called Monté, was twenty-four when he came to Bynner's house. Tall, lean, elegantly handsome in the way of Robert Taylor or Robert Montgomery, with a brisk, debonair walk and an easy way of dressing, wearing clothes so well they seemed insignificant, he had a fine, clear voice, excellent manners, little formal education but a crackling sharp mind, and was well read and intelligent about history, art, and literature. He had tried all kinds of schools and jobs but could "do" nothing, and his patient father, the well-known California architect Myron Hunt, had attempted everything he could think of to help him. He even brought him into his architecture firm, since Bob had superb talents as an architect. Nothing ever took hold.

In the course of his life Hunt published a book of verse; he designed a wing and some rooms for Bynner's house, a mirador and several other changes in the Chapala house, and a living room on the Peter Hurd ranch in San Patricio, New Mexico; and he completely rebuilt a house on Atalaya Hill in Santa Fe, turning it into an exquisite, self-contained structure. He wrote good prose and letters of such brilliant detail and outrageous fun as to be an art in themselves. Yet he never really stayed with anything or did anything—except take care of Hal. Eventually, over the years, as he became more and more bitter, more cynical, and would not stop drinking, smoking, or going out for endless nights on the town, he even failed at times in his care of Hal.

To say he did nothing would be wrong, for he did as much as a good companion does for any writer: he read the poems, edited them, compiled them into books, went over proofs—and he ran the house and took care of the practicalities of their lives. No one would think to fault a woman who did as well. Yet he had to fail because this was his expectation of himself. It was his bitter disgust with himself and his harsh judgment of himself that made what he did unsatisfying. He felt he was, and his best friends knew he was, a talented man who had been indolent, who near the end cared personally only for Hal, for drink, and for some crude sexual experience found in the streets or in public bathrooms, too slight to matter even to him. He knew himself too well to believe in what he did, and he saw human shabbiness in himself and in almost everyone else.

At the beginning this was not so. Bynner found in Bob a fine, handsome companion whose wit was as sharp and whose mind as quick as his own—someone with whom he could easily share, someone who should have a bright future. Bob had a deeply sympathetic and sensitive nature, a desire to love and be loved that must have appealed to Bynner, as it did to so many men and even to some women. For Bob there was a need to look up to someone, to be helped and dealt with in a paternal manner, to be directed in his wayward pattern, and this Bynner could gracefully do.

Their relationship was a marriage, in the sense that we mean a sharing together in life. We do not always know what forces of love bring people together, what collaboration is made to protect weaknesses, what is given and taken. We know so little of the private agreements by which people make their lives that the external pattern of couples often seems inexplicable. Bynner provided the young Hunt with a place to live well, perhaps a place in which to hide; he also provided the kind of stability that might allow Hunt to try for self-fulfillment. In turn, Hunt brought the lively, bright companionship and the flattery of youth that Bynner needed.

WB with his two Indian friends, Patricio Calabaza and Rafael Lovato, stand-
ing in front of WB's house in Santa Fe in 1922.

WB's mother in Santa Fe outside WB's house, and with her son by the front door, 1922. Photographs here and of the Lawrences are by WB or Willard "Spud" Johnson.

WB, Frieda (1879–1956), and D. H. Lawrence (1885–1930) outside WB's house on September 11, 1922, the Lawrences' first day in New Mexico.

Frieda, WB, and Spud at the door to WB's
house, again on September 11, 1922.

D. H. and Frieda Lawrence in Mexico in 1923.

D. H. Lawrence on a canoe on Lake Chapala in Mexico, 1923. The trip to Mexico is included as a part of *The Plumed Serpent* and is the basis of WB's *Journey with Genius*.

Lynn Riggs (1899–1954) in Santa Fe, where he came to visit WB and to serve briefly as his secretary. Later Riggs would write *Green Grow the Lilacs,* on which the musical *Oklahoma* was based.

Rita Padilla (?–1963), WB's housekeeper for almost forty years.

(*Opposite*) Louisa Pugh (1881–1962), WB, and Clifford McCarthy (1904–1968), painted by Russell Cheney (1881–1945) in December 1929. Cheney was a close friend of F. O. Mathiessen (1902–1950), the Harvard scholar of American literature. The two visited WB in Santa Fe. Pugh was a neighbor and close friend. McCarthy was WB's secretary for a short period.

Margreth Mather
(1885–1952), an impor-
tant photographer in
Los Angeles, took this
picture in 1928.

Edna St. Vincent Millay at
Steepletop, her home in Austerlitz,
New York. Photograph by WB
sometime in the 1930s.

Robert Hunt in Mexico in the early
1930s, just after he and Bynner had
begun to live together.

Hunt and Gladys (1890–1973) and Arthur Ficke, likely in Chapala in 1935.

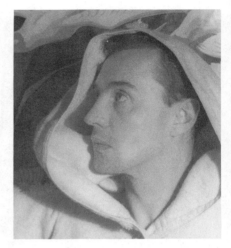

(*Opposite page and above*) Hunt photographed by Carl Van Vechten in New York in December 1937. Reproduced by permission of the Estate of Carl Van Vechten, Joseph Solomon, executor.

WB's house in Santa Fe showing the eclectic mixture of styles. Photo courtesy John Meigs.

(*Opposite*) Henriette Wyeth Hurd (1907–), daughter of the illustrator-artist N. C. Wyeth (1882–1945), sister of Andrew Wyeth (1917–), and wife of Peter Hurd (1904–1984), painted WB in September 1939 in ten days of sittings. It was said that Bynner was painted in the same pose as Whistler's mother. The portrait hangs in the Roswell Museum in New Mexico.

Carl Van Vechten's
photograph of WB taken
in New York in January
1933. Reproduced by
permission of the Estate
of Carl Van Vechten,
Joseph Solomon,
executor.

WB bought a house in Chapala in 1940 and Hunt restored it and built an extensive terrace on the roof. The house was on the square, a short walk from the lake, but its interest centered on the patios, and especially the terraces, with their remarkable views of the mountains and the lake.

(*Opposite*) Ysidoro serves WB breakfast in the Chapala house at some time in the early 1940s, when Bynner was working on his version of Laotzu.

Ysidoro Pulido (1907?–1956) was WB's majordomo for the house in Chapala. They met on WB's first visit in 1923 and remained friends for life. WB even built Pulido's family a house behind his own. Here is Ysidoro in the early 1940s with his mother, wife, and children on one of the terraces of the Chapala house.

Ansel Adams (1902–1984) photographed WB in Santa
Fe in 1951.

WB at his desk in 1956 at seventy-five; note the various Indian and Chinese objects.

WB after his stroke in 1965. There was an effort to make it appear that WB was still active and aware of his situation, but this was not the case.

WB's house on Buena Vista, as it appeared in 1977, nine years after Bynner's death.

A stone Mexican dog marks the place where WB's and Hunt's ashes are buried in the garden of the house Hunt restored on Atalaya Hill in Santa Fe.

If in time Bynner grew old and blind and depended on Hunt, Hunt had nothing else in his life but that now-very-old man who needed him to make the journey up the stairs. If their relationship was based upon a real love and upon deep needs and insecurities, upon an ever-changing hunger for help and support, we are only saying of it what might be said of many relations.

Bynner wrote the following to Hunt in 1934; it reveals important aspects of their relationship. It speaks about Hunt's character and Bynner's needs, but also reveals Bynner's somewhat self-conscious way of dealing with each, as if his Bostonian formality could never quite be lost, even in the privacy of his greatest love:

> I find this written on the back of a telegram.
> "I know now why I love you. Because you are completely clear, straight, sweet, and animal as we all are. You pretend nothing and you are to me everything."
> Not bad!

———

The arrival of Hunt and the publication of *Eden Tree* (which Bynner dedicated to Hunt) declared to Bynner's personal world and his public one that he was most probably homosexual. This was not a common statement for his time or for someone of his position. It could be construed as a bold act. Bynner and Hunt led a married life when this was not largely or even minimally accepted, and Bynner declared his love in his art at a time when it was easy for people to scorn or ignore his work because he was homosexual. Writing about *Eden Tree,* Bynner said: "I am relieved that its honesty has been understood. I am sick of literary glazing over the truth. Most writers do it. Poets, at any rate, shouldn't. So much the Chinese have taught me."

It is impossible to say what effect all of this had on Bynner, Hunt, and the career. Bynner never in writing nor in any recorded conversation made reference to the effect on his career of acknowledging his homosexuality, and he would have been too careful and correct to do so. There is no specific evidence that this revelation of his sexual preference ever affected his career. One's best judgment is that it was another factor that permitted people and critics to ignore Bynner and his work if they chose to do so, before the time when it became possible to recognize an individual or a writer's work for this very reason. It may be that it isolated Bynner from major creative people, but it is also true that he had succeeded in doing that himself, professionally and personally. He might have considered that his sexual nature forced isolation upon him, if he ever went so far as to analyze the matter. The impression one has is that what it meant to be homosexual was something Bynner never analyzed in any serious way. He accepted it, when he finally did, as he accepted so much in life. His homosexuality was another fact of life with which to live. *Eden Tree* was as far as he could go in understanding and expressing the issue. For its time, *Eden Tree* might be considered very far to go: in general, the subject of being "gay" was not seriously presented or publicly discussed in most American literary or social worlds.

≡

Throughout the thirties there was some shortage of money in Bynner's life, but nothing serious. The inheritance from his stepsister was well invested and his mother was generous to him. He and Hunt could generally do what they wanted. They traveled to and from New York, to the West Coast, and to Mexico. The extremes of their new life together can be seen in these letters, the first by Bynner to his mother in February 1932 and the second by Hunt to Paul Horgan in June of the same year:

Incidentally . . . I have seen a good deal of Serge Eisenstein, the Russian movie director about whom you must have read in *The New Republic* and elsewhere. He has been thirteen months making a picture of Mexican life [which eventually appeared in 1933 as *Thunder over Mexico* but was also edited in 1939 as *In the Sun* and often called *Qué Viva Mexico*]. Twice I have watched him taking his shots and several times have spent hours talking with him. He seems to me to have something of the rare quality called genius. And he has an extraordinary staff. He takes his pictures in the actual street and landscape of Mexico, picking his actors spontaneously from the watching crowd. . .

Just back from California. I went out on the spur of the moment and came back on a shoestring, as it were . . . and still am getting my breath from the madness of it all, and the depression. Such a world! Really, I know nothing anymore, not that I ever did . . . but WHAT are we coming to what with Lindbergh babies, airplanes going over 400 miles per hour, Jimmy Walker, the bonus seekers on the steps of the capitol, tear-gas bombs, the stock market, the Japs in Manchuria, breadlines, papal encyclicals, assassins, speakeasies, plagues, the radio, Mother India, SEX and the Austin Car? I *ASK* you? Mercy! In order to be stylish (nothing more I assure you) I have decided to tune my mood to the times and be really despondent, but to do it pleasantly. Hence, I have gone on the wagon and given up cigarettes . . . and can now mourn and mope with the best of them. Oh dear. . . .

Bynner continued to work throughout this period. He discovered the unpublished poems of Frederick Goddard Tuckerman and edited them in 1931. His next book was a tour de force: seventy sonnets, each on a friend or acquaintance, focusing on what made him or her a type or of a certain class. These *Guest Book* poems have such titles as "Debutante," "Hostess," "Communist," "Bluestocking," "Widower," "Playboy." Bynner included his famous friends and some not so famous, although none are named; he wrote about himself, Paul Thévenaz, Robert Hunt (as "Chantecleer," "Ganymede," and "Lucifer"), Lady Duff-Twysden (the model for Brett Ashley) and her husband, Clinton King (as "Expatriates"), Mabel Dodge Luhan, Robinson Jeffers, Edna Millay, Amy Lowell, Carl Van Vechten, Thornton Wilder, and Max Eastman. *Guest Book* was meant to be read lightly, for fun, but unfortunately it provoked some bitter remarks from people who thought they recognized themselves. Like Spectra, it was another occasion when Bynner used humor to distance himself and caused others to feel uncomfortable, to wonder if he could be trusted.

Hunt chose a group of Bynner's poems, and these appeared in 1936, with an introduction by Paul Horgan, as *Selected Poems*. They were not ignored, but they did not achieve what a man of fifty-five had hoped a survey of his life's work would suggest—important critical attention, perhaps even a prize. By this time he could see that he would never reach the level of recognition he sought, that the world of poetry had begun to pass him by, even to forget him. *Selected Poems* suggests that even Bynner might be losing a sense of his finest voice. It included too many of his weaker lyrics, only three of the Spectra poems, and none of the Chinese translations. Hunt excluded the Spectra poems because they were "too far a cry from the general manner and meaning of the book, too disconcerting a break in the mood." Without Spectra or the translations, a critic looking at the work might easily wonder what made Bynner distinctive.

An incident with Robert Frost suggests how deeply Bynner's lack of recognition was affecting him. They had been friends from the early twenties, and at one point Frost had agreed to write the introduction to a volume of Bynner's verse, something he finally did not do. As Frost won acceptance and became over the years the beloved poet of the American people, Bynner began to resent that Frost had succeeded where he had not. No role as poet would have pleased Bynner more than the one Frost was assuming. Also, while Bynner's poetry was decidedly different from Frost's, it was closer to Frost's than to the work of any other contemporary, with one possible exception of aspects of William Carlos Williams. When, in 1935, Frost came to Santa Fe to speak, Bynner was to introduce him but arrived late; Frost had already begun. The next day Frost was taken to see one of the pueblos and arrived late at Bynner's for lunch. They discussed a book of poems by Horatio Colony that Bynner liked but Frost found "bestial." Without any apparent provocation, Bynner poured his glass of beer on Frost's head. After a stunned moment, the incident was passed over—at least Frost said nothing and Bynner did nothing more. Later Bynner wrote an apology; in it he turned the incident into a kind of joke, but one that he said had misfired. It was a lame attempt to cover his anger and must have sounded insufficient even to Bynner.

Many years later Bynner was at the Hanover Inn in New Hampshire and saw Frost in the dining room. He went over to him and said, "Robert, do you remember me? I apologize for pouring that beer on you." Frost looked at him in silence for a brief moment, as if, Bynner felt, taking his measure, and then recited two of Bynner's poems. A great compliment had been paid that was always to amaze Bynner.

In 1963 Bynner wrote a poem in honor of Frost. Although it must have hurt him to know that he lacked Frost's genius, he had accepted his limitations, and within them he did well what he did. He had reached the point where he was content to accept a less public acknowledgment of his own worth.

Robert Frost
(1874–1963)

They would have stayed there for farewell
Until the train pulled out
But he waved them away and they could tell
He knew what he was about.

The train held only strangers, yes,
But he was a stranger too—
When you say goodbye to friends who bless
They leave you only you.

———

On November 25, 1937, Mrs. Wellington, Bynner's mother, died in her apartment in New York at the age of seventy-nine. She had been headstrong and not always wise in some actions in her life, but she had been confronted with hard conditions that often made judgment difficult. She created many of her own problems by demanding too much and never being satisfied with anything. The great passion of her life was her poet son, and when he, against her advice, moved away from her, she was too proud to accept his suggestion that she come to live in Santa Fe. He could describe her objectively, but never without great feeling. She was, she knew, the single greatest element in his life. He wrote of her in 1929 in *Indian Earth*, when he was almost fifty:

To My Mother concerning a Chapala Sunset

To you, at evening, I exclaim aloud—
Why have you never seen the range of light
That lives along Chapala mountain-tops
With massive interchange of sun and moon?
And yet, before I was born, you had often watched,
On mountain-clouds as beautiful as these,
Changes of light that I shall never see
In this confused and separating world.

She had flown to Mexico City on December 11, 1936, and toured so energetically that Bynner and Hunt were exhausted. They went to Chapala and stayed at the hotel on the water, a grand wreck of a place owned by an ancient eccentric, doña María Pacheco viuda de Arzapalo, who dressed in lavender and white silk and dined once a week with Mrs. Wellington, the two talking endlessly each in her own language, which the other could not speak. Mrs. Wellington admired doña María's ability to talk without pausing, an accomplishment she was known to possess herself, and she said of doña María what she wanted thought of herself: "She is wonderful and a constant source of interest and astonishment to me."

She and Hunt did not get on. As Bynner said, there was no hope, for his mother was determined that they fight, and the politer Hunt was, the worse she acted. She objected to the jerseys men wore in Mexico and called them undershirts: "Men don't seem to realize that the less they show of themselves, the less they look like baboons." She had a way of directing these offhand remarks at Hunt. On their journey north to Santa Fe, she accused him of deliberately jolting her by driving the car roughly. Bynner recorded an incident on one day of that journey: "During this final day in Mexico she took to pelting Bob's head or mine or the car generally with tangerine peels accompanied by peals of laughter—hours of this perverse pastime, which I should like to see anyone play for a moment in her own car." She saw herself being replaced and could not tolerate it, but her need for attention forced her to remain in Santa Fe. Finally she said she found it all "forlorn" and flew back to New York on March 31. Bynner wrote of her visit: "She had almost ground us into dead dust. She knew it and was glad. But what a sad gladness she had always made for herself out of life is told in her diary with its almost daily dark entries."

In October her depressions grew worse and were more frequently noted in her journal. Her face began to pain her, a symptom that she noted again and again. Bynner arrived in New York just before she died. His secretary for many years, Henriette Harris, recorded Mrs. Wellington's death in her journal as Bynner later described it.

He told about the last hours around her, how active her mind was to the very end. As Tim and he were sitting with her, and she was suffering, Tim put his hand on hers and said, to her, "Poor woman . . . take it easy . . ." She turned on him with her old vehemence and said, "How dare you talk like that to me—how can I take it easy, when I don't know what I'm taking!!" Hal said those were almost her last words. A little later, with the doctor there, she suddenly sat up in bed and threw off the covers with strength and said, "Let me up? I have an errand . . ." And when they gently made her lie down again, she looked around at them all, and said, almost to herself, and over and over again, "Well, well, well . . . Well, well, well . . ." Hal went on to say that she had made the request several times that once she was in her coffin, to let no one see her, to "just nail me in immediately," and so he was troubled as to what to do at the funeral. When a cousin came in for the funeral and told him of that same request made to her, he appealed to the undertaker, who said, "Why don't you just leave her in her bed for the two days?" Which was done. "I was in that great apartment with her alone for two nights, not the least bit disturbed. We had to pass back and forth through her room, to the bathroom, and through her room to another room, and there she was, just resting—a person amongst us."

Bynner asked Hunt to come to New York right after his mother's death and they arranged to ship back much of her furniture and many objects and paintings. Bynner also inherited a large sum of money. They returned to Santa Fe and their life continued, in appearance, much as it had before. It was a year later that Bob Hunt pointed out to Bynner that he had not written any poetry since his mother's death and said that it was now time to begin. When Bynner let this pass, Hunt went out and bought him a writing pad and pencil. Bynner simply began again, and in 1940 his next volumes of poems, *Against the Cold,* appeared; many were about age and death. One of these poems is a condensation of emotion in Bynner's most delicate lyrical style, in which, as in Chinese poetry, every word tells. It is called "Spring and a Mother Dead."

> I who should write her epitaph
> Would err:
> What could I say to anyone
> But her?
>
> Apricot-blossoms open
> Like a bell:
> But this time there is nobody
> To tell.

Mrs. Wellington and her older son were very much alike: single-minded, intelligent, humorous, outrageous at times, obsessive, often depressed. They left their mark on one another. The relationship between mother and son had been a deeply creative and destructive link that did not end with death. Bynner never escaped the frightening sense that what he loved most was also what wanted most to control and limit him. It was as though he continually fled what most deeply attracted him.

═══

The legacy from his mother and her family, and his father's, had to affect Bynner. On the one hand, she and the families were a positive influence: they gave him the ability to look clearly at the world and a genuine sense of a life different from the ordinary. On the other, they gave him an erratic and unstable nervous system and with it a debilitatingly uncertain sense of who he should be. These conditions affected various aspects of his life, but none more significantly than his relationships with people and his sexual orientation. There was in Bynner some deep reservoir of frustration and uncertainty. These elements appear quite directly in two of his poems, and the poems reveal important aspects of Bynner.

If it is in *Eden Tree,* as has been stated, that Bynner acknowledges his homosexuality, it is here also that he speaks of its "seal / Of double solitude." This acknowledgment and reservation represent important aspects of Bynner. They are expressed directly in section XXVI of the poem.

Bewilderedly
He thought of Jonathan, he thought of Paul . . .
Why had men always entered where women should be,
He asked himself and in asking tried to be just.
He was drunk, he was clear, he was open, dispassionate, wise.
Why, when women were soft and intelligent bringers of ease,
Why, when women were women and shaped to the need of a male,
Why, when women were pale
As the snow on a mountain that made his awakening eyes
Content to awaken,
Should he be shaken
By the hard visage of a man confronting his?
What was all this?

I find you, Jonathan, unshaved, but dear
Beside me in my bed. I love you here.
Women are women. Women have need
Of Adam and his seed;
But men, when men love Adam, are the touch
Of God's hand on Adam. There is much
To be told about this that Eve would rather not hear.
It is no mere
Denial of Life, it is something else than a loss
Of life on an immolating cross;
It is something real,
With no generation or brood:
It is the seal
Of double solitude.

The passage seems to exalt the love between men and to consider that it leads only to the condition of solitude. This concept must be understood in relation to the entire poem. *Eden Tree* is an autobiographical exploration of a man's encounters with many forms of love, religion, and human experience, encounters that lead the man, called Adam in the poem, to realize that there are for him no traditional or experimental ways to transcend the meaningless he sees in life. Life is an experience without definitive meaning, if one truly looks at it. This terrifying reality cannot be avoided, only accepted. The figure in the poem accepts life as it is and resigns himself to isolation as the essential human condition. The poem expresses Bynner's feelings of distance and loss, even in homosexuality where the loss seems, to Bynner, a double solitude. Bynner's deep sense of being separate from others and unable to relate to people is at the center of the poem's vision, and being homosexual reinforces this isolation.

It is worth remembering that *Eden Tree* was published in 1931, just after Hunt came to live with Bynner, and only partially reflects this relationship. At the same time, it should be remembered that Bynner extensively rewrote it in 1936 and the entire poem was included in *Selected Poems,* a volume edited by Hunt. No matter what Hunt meant to him, the relationship could not overcome Bynner's deep sense of being isolated and his sense that if one looked clearly at life, nothing in life could give any permanent meaning, anyway to withstand the overwhelming reality of isolation and death.

Another poem presents a complicated story, one less attractive in what it says about Bynner, but a story that reveals a great deal about him and especially about his homosexual relationships. "Episode of Decay" was written in the late thirties, and Bynner stated that it is about two friends, Haniel and Alice Long. The poem describes how a husband allows his wife to destroy him, literally to eat him alive. It is a story told with a rich and delightful sense of black humor.

Being very religious, she devoted most of her time to fear.
Under her calm visage, terror held her,
Terror of water, of air, of earth, of thought,
Terror lest she be disturbed in her routine of eating her husband.
She fattened on his decay, but she would let him decay without pain.
And still she would ask, as she consumed him particle by particle,
Do you wish me to take it, dear? Will it make you happier?
And down the plump throat he went day after day in tid-bits;
And he mistook the drain for happiness,
Could hardly live without the deadly nibbling. . . .
She had eaten away the core of him under the shell,
Eaten his heart and drunk away his breath;
Till on Saturday, the seventeenth of April,
She made her breakfast on an edge of his mind.
He was very quiet that day, without knowing why.
A last valiant cell of his mind may have been insisting that the fault
   was not hers but his;
But soon he resumed a numbness of content:
The little cell may have been thinking that one dies sooner or later
And that one's death may as well be useful. . . .
For supper, he offered her tea and cake from behind his left ear;
And after supper they took together the walk they always took together
   after supper.

Haniel Long, the acknowledged source for this poem, was born in Burma in 1388. The son of a Methodist missionary, Long went to Phillips Exeter and to Harvard, where Bynner met him in 1908. It is clear from the many extant letters that they were close literary associates, good friends, and lovers at least for a period at the start, and perhaps at various times thereafter. It is the kind of relationship in which the evident pleasure expressed on both sides indicates the deepest kind of attraction.

Long was a slight and reticent man of great sensitivity and a highly independent vision. He may have opened himself to Bynner because of Bynner's strong and outgoing nature, or he may have wanted a father figure to guide his life and career. It is clear that they shared literary interests, especially a deep interest in Walt Whitman and American literature and eventually their common interest in Asian culture. They went on to share their great respect for the Native American cultures of the Southwest and Mexico. Although very different men, they both looked at the world with strong, individualistic visions and with broadly conceived interests, including interests in cultures not usually acknowledged at that time.

Long was to write several works that are little known today but that are original, provocative, and worthy of attention. Particularly interesting is his account of the Spanish explorer Alvar Nuñez Cabeza de Vaca (c. 1490-c. 1557), who came to the North American continent in 1528, was shipwrecked on the Gulf Coast near Galveston, and had to walk across the Southwest with the support of only two other Spaniards, a black Moroccan slave, Esteban, and the Indians they met along the way. Cabeza de Vaca wrote an official report to the king of this eight-year journey after he arrived in Mexico City in 1536 (published in 1542). Long's version presents what Cabeza de Vaca did not say about the white man's experiences with the so-called savages and their pagan religion—with men who kept him alive and showed him a new world, not only a physical one but also a spiritual one. The book presents the human goodness in those considered evil, the prejudice and arrogance of the Christian, and the dilemma of the good man who stands between these worlds. Long called it *Interlinear to Cabeza de Vaca* (1936), or what actually occurred: what came between the lines of the official report. It is an amazingly insightful and important book that Henry Miller wrote about with great interest. In *A World of Light* (1976), May Sarton also praised it in her description of the Longs, whom she knew well and admired. In later editions the book has been called *The Marvelous Adventure of Cabeza de Vaca* and *The Power Within Us*.

This is only one of several books Long wrote, at least two others of which seem as original and as interesting as this one. *Pittsburgh Memo-*

randa (1935) is the account of a group of men from that city and is concerned with the way a place, an environment, shapes our character. The issues here are quite unusual for the time Long wrote. The individuals include Carnegie, Frick, and Stephen Foster, as well as other, lesser known people. The other book is *Malinche (Doña Marina)* (1939), the story of the Yucatán woman who became Cortés's mistress, betrayed her people for his love, and then saw how he and the Spaniards destroyed her people.

Long taught English for many years at what was then called the Carnegie Institute of Technology in Pittsburgh. He married in 1913. In the late twenties he had a severe breakdown, the cause of which is unclear, but his father had twice been forced to leave positions because of his mental and physical health, and Haniel had inherited his weak and sensitive nature. After several extended visits alone to Santa Fe to see how it affected his health, visits that he usually spent with Bynner, he decided to move there in the early thirties. Bynner was clearly an influence in the decision to move.

Long's marriage was something that had deeply disturbed Bynner and something he could never fully accept. Alice Long was an educated, well-traveled woman and, unusual for her time, had been to Asia and was knowledgeable about it, but Bynner found her comic and limited. It is true she spoke in a high baby voice and was exceedingly fat, and others did find her character amusing, but she was considered by most people a bright, thoughtful person. The real point seems to be that in marrying her, Long had rejected Bynner, as Long would over the years reject Bynner's artistic influence and go in a direction decidedly different from Bynner's. Bynner might well have felt that Long was denying his true nature in marrying. For all of this, he held Alice responsible and was venomous in his comments about her. Bob Hunt also disliked Alice Long and was jealous of Haniel Long's powerful influence on Bynner. It is a recognition of that influence and the power of Bynner's feeling for Long that "Episode of Decay" was published in *Against the Cold* in 1940, some 33 years after Bynner had met Long, some 27 years after Long had married Alice, and 10 years after Bynner had found the man he claimed he most loved. Clearly Bynner could not escape from or deal well with what remained a life-long attachment and an inaccessible love.

This whole relationship ends as confusingly as one might expect. In 1948, at a dinner party for several people, Hunt became very drunk and abusive about Jews, a subject about which he could be excessively unpleasant. Although Bynner's brother was married to a Jewish woman, and his secretary for many years and close friend, Henriette Harris, to whom he dedicated *Against the Cold,* was Jewish, Bynner at best passively accepted such remarks and could himself even make them. The Longs and the other guests were so upset by what occurred that they refused ever to see Bynner again. This incident was the single most disturbing social experience of Bynner's life. It hung in his mind like some dead carcass and he returned to it again and again, but he was unable to get rid of it.

Bynner and Long were finally brought together on Bynner's seventy-fifth birthday, on August 10, 1956, both men ill and with little sight. It was a correct but superficial reconciliation that never addressed any of the life-long issues that were involved. Alice Long was not at the party because she was ill, or so it was said. She died on October 14 in Santa Fe and Haniel Long on October 17 at the Mayo Clinic in Rochester, Minnesota, where he had gone for special treatment. Bynner was asked to read Long's poetry at the joint funeral for the Longs, which he did as if their relationship had been restored to what it once had been. The question, of course, is what that relation truly was.

Perhaps "Episode of Decay" and the relationship with the Longs says less about Bynner's homosexuality than about the complexity of love and human relations, and in particular about Bynner's struggle to deal with them. What can one discover from the poem and the incident? In part, they are expressions of Bynner's fear of intimacy, of approaching and dealing with the more complex aspects of human experience and his own sexuality. They are also an expression of how Bynner could choose humor (even venomous humor) to deal with a subject too powerful for him to address directly—and it is well to think how often he used humor in this way. The poem shows how Bynner could reconstruct situations that might otherwise cause the depression that overwhelmed so many in his family.

Yet it is also true that the poem and the relationship show how willing he was to bring his life into his poetry, even if, at times, through the disguise of humor. If he could be slight or too quickly seek the pleasant, as D. H. Lawrence correctly believed, Bynner did have a great capacity to accept the various aspects of his life and to let them appear openly to others. Largely speaking, he was what he appeared to be and in this was a man whose character was unusual. It is worth repeating here a remark he wrote in his journal: "A. E. Housman wished his light verse and his many variants destroyed. Willa Cather forbade printing any of her letters. I cannot imagine fear of letting people see one's frivolities or stupidities. Why always a cravat?" It seems that Bynner—perhaps with bravado, perhaps through fear of probing into his nature, perhaps with an awareness of life's complex variety—did not mind letting his truth be told.

≡

When World War II came, Bynner's and Hunt's lives changed, as did everyone's. Bob wanted to serve but was rejected by both army and navy because of his health—his lungs were not good and years of overindulgence had greatly weakened his body. Instead, he served on the local draft board. Bynner was state chairman for New Mexico of the United China Relief Fund. After more than a year with the draft board, Bob was exhausted and wanted to take a vacation; Bynner had been giving a lecture for the United China Relief on "Chinese People and Poetry" and wanted to develop it into a book. On St. Patrick's Day, 1943, he and Hunt left for Chapala. They had bought a house there in 1940 and were making many renovations, especially the building of a high sun terrace at the back of the second floor.

Bynner's brother, Tim, came to Chapala for a brief visit, without his wife. By May, Bob Hunt had left. He felt a need to serve his country and went to San Francisco to work as a checker on the loading docks in the civilian force and later in the navy personnel bureau for the docks. Hunt's work was exhausting, at least to him. He wrote Bynner on August 28 and September 5, 1943:

> I know it's Saturday night in the Big City and all that, but I worked all day—and the other guys have gone out for a spree—but I can no longer even see the keyboard, what with sleeplessness and fatigue. Maybe tomorrow I'll do better by you: this certainly is no letter—and I have in no way expressed to you my thoughts (about the both of us, as it were, and the world in general) but I can no longer stay awake. . . . I only hope that you are well and happy, and working hard—and that you think of me as often as I do of you—and that someday soon we can get together again in more peaceful times. . . . Yes; I'll write again tomorrow. It will be much better . . . good-night, and bless you.

> I've just come off a Liberty Ship—a new one, where I've been "supervising" a loading lot. The ships are fun—and it's interesting to watch all the loading machinery and the great cranes, etc. The men will work all night—my time comes next week, I think. . . . Another interruption: Six freight cars of flour, beer and cigarettes have just come in—so, I'm off. See you later! . . . I wish you could hear some of the language around here. The Navy was calm and tame. *These* guys are really tough (on the outside)—but their off-work hobbies would kill you: knitting, collecting butterflies—and one does miniatures! *Sheer* Compensation. . . I, on the other hand, make sleep my hobby. I've even had to give up what little was left of my so-called Sex-life—if any. Just as well, perhaps, and why not?

Bynner was hard at work on the Chinese book but also active in the social life of Chapala and involved in repairs on the house. A servant and his family were living in a house he had built for them behind his own. As a boy, the man had attached himself to Bynner when the writer first came to Chapala in 1923. Bynner had never come to visit when Ysidoro Pulido did not take charge of his life, and now he was officially in charge, as he and his family would be for the rest of Bynner's life. A young American painter, Charles Stigall, too ill at the time to be drafted, came to Chapala to recuperate and lived in the house with Bynner. Bynner wrote to Hunt about him:

A babyless bachelor won't disrupt the house, and I'll be glad in a way to have a little break in my habit of solitude. He's quiet and will, I think, let me work as much as is good for me. Also it may perk up Ysidoro, who was going a bit slack on the food because of my caring so little.

Hunt wrote Bynner's brother on December 7, 1943:

Lord how I miss him! And how wonderful it will be for us all to be together again one of these fine days. But who knows? I, for one, have given up guessing at anything, and can only hope that we will all be in one piece by the time we all meet again. It's a hell of a life—this being separated and uncertain as to the plans of mice and men—but what to do? And, as you know, I couldn't just vegetate any longer; and this seemed to be the answer. It's certainly better than fox-holes;—and Christ knows I'm not complaining.

Hunt remained in San Francisco until September 1944, when he returned to Chapala, too ill to continue working. He and Bynner did not return to Santa Fe until August 1945. It was during this period, while working on the Chinese book—which was never finished—that Bynner began to write a version of Laotzu based upon other English translations. *The Way of Life according to Laotzu* was published in October 1944 and was to be his most popular work, selling over fifty thousand copies in his lifetime and still being sold. Mistakenly, the Knopfs refused it, thinking it would not be popular, so Bynner sent it to a college friend, Richard Walsh (the husband of Pearl Buck), who ran the John Day Company.

Bynner wanted "an American version," which was used as the translation's subtitle, a version easily accessible to the modern American reader.

In this he succeeded admirably, and the style still very much speaks to the contemporary reader. Translating during the war, when it seemed to him that "the way of life" was being greatly ignored and even destroyed, he hoped his version would redirect readers to the essence of life. At the age of sixty-three, from his Asianlike retreat from civilization, he offered the wisdom of Laotzu in an American voice. Laotzu was for Bynner the quintessential expression of the full democratic spirit, so needed at this time, Bynner believed.

> Laotzu knew that organization and institution interfere with a man's responsibility to himself and therefore with his proper use of life, that the more any outside authority interferes with a man's use of life, and the less the man uses it according to his own instinct and conscience, the worse for the man and the worse for society. The only authority is "the way of life" itself; a man's sense of it is the only priest or prophet.

It is interesting how close this remark about Laotzu is to Bynner's statement on women's suffrage and human freedom, a statement that he wrote in the second decade of the century and that was quoted earlier. Bynner believed in democracy and saw this concept in Laotzu, because it was for him the direction to the "way," to the freedom for someone to find his or her own sense of life.

≡

Bynner was sixty-five years old in 1946, but he had sustained remarkable health and youth. Once he had gone bald, which occurred gradually over the first two decades of the century, his appearance changed little until now, when illness—low blood pressure, a blood clot in his leg, colitis, arthritis—began to disturb him. His friends had begun to die, and his letters comment on the beginning of this isolation. Franklin Roosevelt's death in 1945 was for him a summation of the life of his generation. Arthur Ficke's death in November 1945 was the loss of his oldest and closest friend, a relationship that went back to 1900 and touched all aspects of his life. It was acknowledged that the work going on in Los Alamos, just north of Santa Fe, was with the atom bomb. Bynner was fascinated with the scientists and the bomb but saw reflected in Los Alamos how little he or even Santa Fe had escaped the present destructive world. His secretary, Henriette Harris, had to retire because of back trouble. She was replaced by Dorothy Chauvenet, who would remain to the end of his life. He and Frieda Lawrence celebrated their birthdays together on August 10 and 11 and saw how age had affected each of them. Bynner began to have eye trouble over the next several years, which eventually led to an operation, blindness in one eye, continual pain, and, finally, nearly total blindness.

He went to the West Coast in 1946, ostensibly to get away from the high altitude in Santa Fe, which wasn't good for his heart, but while in Hollywood and San Francisco he was endlessly visiting and meeting people, seeing George Kennedy of the *Hollywood Reporter* and Dr. Hans Fehling, both old friends. At a party a friend admitted he himself had changed, but "Hal is but slightly changed, if at all. He did a great deal of talking and kept things quite lively." Bynner left for Chapala just before Christmas of 1946 with a severe case of eczema that bothered him for several months, making writing difficult: "And I have been slow these days with new writing. Rhythms don't float through me as happily as they used to." But by March 1947 another book of verse had appeared, *Take Away the Darkness*. It is a book of lyrics that address the recent darkness of the war and the encroaching darkness of age with directness and gentleness.

Dead in the Philippines

Dead in the Philippines are they . . .
These boys who, born in Santa Fe,
Spoke Spanish here, spoke Spanish there,
Have now no language anywhere—

Save as the dead speak after death,
With an acute mysterious breath
At sudden times of night and day,
Some of the things they used to say.

The Two Windows

Out of my western window,
The purple clouds are dying
Edged with fire;
And out of my eastern window,
The full round moon is rising
Formed of ice.

So beautiful,
Although the day go by

And the night come on forever,
Is this momentary world.

If there was a slowing down, a serenity, and an acceptance in Bynner, in Hunt there was the beginning of bitterness. Even Bynner acknowledged it in writing a friend: "I can't help feeling that he is developing a genius for unnecessary quarrels. . . . His opinion should be his of course but might be governed to make life easier all around." Hunt seemed to have exhausted himself in the war and had little left to give. He worked on the Santa Fe and Chapala houses and soon on the house he himself bought in Santa Fe, but most of his energy went into drinking and sex. Everywhere he went, he carried his own case of liquor, containing bourbon, gin, and rum; he was often very drunk, and Bynner worried about his safety. If he agreed to go to a dinner party, he often became so drunk and belligerent that he provoked strong reactions. It was at the dinner in 1948, referred to earlier, that Hunt's abusive language in reference to Jews, and Bynner's attempted defense of him, lost them the friendship of several people, one of them the poet Haniel Long. Bynner was a man who had learned to accept a great deal and who wanted to avoid conflict—in many ways he had become Taoist in his reaction to life—but Hunt had become a force working against acceptance and tolerance. A tender man grown bitter, Hunt was capable of strong feelings of love and anger—perhaps even more so than Bynner—but was now a potential source of chaos. The pressure on Bynner grew as Hunt became more difficult. Bynner never spoke against him, never showed any anger or hostility in public, but to his closest friends he expressed a frightened concern that Bob would be lost. Bynner described the relationship in terms that are perceptive and disturbing:

Bob just looked into the room. It's four a.m. Pleasant creatures have gone their way, from his evening and from mine, separate. He had disturbances in his, I only strangeness and age to disturb mine. But he says in the doorway, hearing the typewriter: "Do I disturb your style?" I wonder why that peculiar wickedness in Bob? Except that I know. He is always a little jealous of my connecting with others—or even with myself. And of course I treasure that jealousy.

Sometimes I think I know what it is all about: that in Bob I have captured the beauty of evil and that he, hating cats, has a feline consciousness of that curious fact in our relationship and likes it: that it relieves him of being evil. But to no one except you could I ever try to express the strange and finally beautiful fact: our two beings, adverse but mutually needed, making sound fact and liking it. Either of us without the other would be insincere, incomplete. We correct each other's lies. It's a good team and, by some happy chance, a respectful and comfortable team blessed with the boon of warmth. We are lucky and—now I am sententious—we owe, because of our luck, a lot of patience.

Such a life is not lived without a price. Bynner's aging, with its many losses and illnesses, the lack of recognition for his years of writing, and his problems with Bob—all these had to affect him. Eventually he developed a serious case of shingles on his shoulders, which lasted for many years and was probably stress related. His friends began to see a great isolating egotism, as if he were ignoring everything but what he chose to see, yet perhaps it was that he had not the stamina to focus on life. Henriette Harris wrote: "When we see him as we did last night, I wonder. He didn't ask any of us one thing about ourselves. But there is something about him we love, I guess, and perhaps just take it and forget the rest. I hope the evening fed him." There was little time, little energy, for anything but himself and the act of performing well for a special few.

≡

Having finished a new book of verse, Bynner went with Bob to the East Coast in 1947, for the first time in a decade, to see many friends—Edna Millay and her husband, Alfred and Blanche Knopf, William Rose Benét, Robert Flaherty, Ezra Pound at St. Elizabeths Hospital in Washington, who greeted Bynner with a great bear hug, and other friends on down the coast and across the Gulf. Bynner left at once for Chapala; Hunt visited his family in Los Angeles before joining him. They returned to Santa Fe, where they saw the poet Stephen Spender, the actress Jane Cowl, the painters Peter and Henriette Wyeth Hurd, Frieda Lawrence, and the heiress and art collector Millicent Rogers. Then they were off to New York again to hear the pianist and composer Victor Babin's song cycle, based upon Bynner poems, which was performed at Town Hall; and then to Key West, where Bynner's old friend John Dewey lent them a house. After he returned to Santa Fe, Bynner had his first slight heart attack in February 1949, nothing serious, but enough to force him to reduce his pace considerably. They returned to Chapala in late February to rest, but it was then that Bynner's severe eye problems began.

Thinking they both needed diversion, and not having been to Europe in almost fifty years, Bynner began a six-month trip, starting in January 1950, to Egypt, Greece, North Africa, and Europe with Hunt, an old friend, Clinton King, and his wife, Narcissa. On this trip they visited Jane Bowles, Alice B. Toklas, Thornton Wilder, and James Baldwin in Paris; Sybille Bedford and George Santayana in Rome—the latter twice at the Convent of the Blue Sisters where he lived; Norman Douglas in Capri; and Osbert Sitwell, John Strachey, Arthur Waley, and Alfred Noyes in England. His journal of the trip included incisive portraits of these people. Here is the entry for Thursday, April 13, after he had visited Alice B. Toklas:

> We have tea with Alice B. Toklas and the famous white poodle (the third, I believe) named Basket, at 5 rue Christine. She is an open-faced kindly old dame whose mannish banged hair-cut, decisive nose and gray moustache only add to the gentleness of her eyes and speech. When I said, however, that my relations with Mabel Dodge Luhan were alternately on and off, she remarked: "Ours were on once, then off for good. Her schemings are meaningless. And so is she." The poor lady looked lone in her cold apartment among the Picassos etc. and said she longed for the U.S.A. and its good food and smaller landscapes, not liking the wide-open landscapes of the Southwest and California. But the die had been cast for her by Gertrude Stein—and in Paris she will stay now till the end. Travel is too difficult for her with the poodle, or even visiting friends in France. "I hope that our lives will terminate together. I tried to arrange it ahead with the veterinarian, but the French do not like that sort of thing—and he brushed my arrangement aside." She told how the Germans, just before the liberation took from the apartment silver and china wrapped in the best linen, and how Gertrude Stein would not let her list it for recovery. "That's over," said G.S.

That fall, back in Santa Fe, Bynner entertained the Igor Stravinskys, Aldous Huxley, Robert Oppenheimer, Christopher Isherwood, Carl Van Vechten, Martha Graham, Ina Claire, Richard Arlen, and Clara Bow—a list he delighted in reciting to other visitors. His young friend Miranda Masocco, who ran one of the best shops on the plaza in Santa Fe, brought many of these people to his house and kept his life as active as was possible. That fall he had his first severe heart attack, and in June 1951 he had the eye operation that failed to prevent the eventual loss of sight in one eye. Yet there is no indication that Bynner had decided to stop; he continued to go regularly to Chapala and the West Coast, especially to see an eye doctor, and he returned to Europe in 1952 to visit Portugal, Spain, France, and Italy, and in 1957, Greece. He wrote this message to himself in 1951 on the eve of his seventieth birthday, a message that expresses a great deal about his life and his point of acceptance. He was still very much alive.

When a man has reached seventy, he has lived his natural life and ought to be able to begin to use it. At least he can look around him and without fear or favor face the truth.

In my own province what do I see? I see English poetry dominated too long by a eunuch. T. S. Eliot laughed at an aunt long since for depending upon *The Boston Evening Transcript* and forthwith he proceeded himself to become, for all the little aunts of literature, *The Boston Evening Transcript*. Somehow he has contrived to sterilize poetry for a quarter century, to nod his nicely glazed toy head and seem a sage mandarin.

I visit Santayana, still sitting in Rome. He repudiates his *Life of Reason*—except for one part of it. I wish I could remember which part; but I felt, when he told me which, that he treasured it still, not so much for its content as because it had been magically realized in words. Technique, immensely important. since the same thoughts running in many men need creative expression to reach open life, is nevertheless not quite all, as William Carlos Williams wrote me he nearly believed it to be. The peril is that expression for its own sake tends to become mechanism. There was for me once in the harsh wooden seat-rub of a privy a comfort which enameled plumbing cannot give.

Yes, this is the day for me, the edge of my seventieth year. Such days have come and gone for billions but this is the day for me, when my life, by biblical calculation, should be finished and, by my own, should begin. Once more I say in my heart: You have lived your life, now use it; you have spent it, now earn it. And I feel a clutch at the throat of what breath is left me, realizing that my breath still blows away like the down of a dandelion or the airy spokes of any day's sun. But there is sudden exhilaration too. I am free. I have lived and not died and the space between life and death feels like an eternal space in which not only to continue but to begin as with new youth; small lungs full of all breath, small fingers probing all touch, small eyes focusing infinity, but with the reach of human living behind me as well as ahead of me, made into a new youth and a stronger honesty, with a fuller warmth of everlasting responsibility. At first responsive, now responsible. Though there be gaps in the plumes, there is a sweet preening of old wings. I can still fly. And how often do you find a dead bird?

Journey With Genius was published in 1951, just at the time of his seventieth birthday. It is a personal reflection made in age of a period almost thirty years earlier, and it was and remains a controversial book. Alfred Knopf had refused it because he thought it too long with too much criticism, but the real reason may be that the book went against the grain of current literary opinion. John Day, who had published *The Way of Life,* accepted the Lawrence book.

Bynner's book has faults, perhaps the worst being its length and his too-insistent making of points, but, as mentioned earlier, it was one of the first efforts to see Lawrence whole and to deal with him and his writing in a somewhat less reverential way. What emerges is the dark, demanding, and hero-driven Lawrence; the optimistic, engaging, and democratic Bynner. They seem to represent two divergent sensibilities that have appeared in literature in this century. Bynner does not force this point, nor should it be simplified in explanation, but the character of the two writers emerges with considerable symbolic implications that suggest polarities we have begun to consider in the major writers of this century. Bynner clearly places Lawrence with Pound, Eliot, and Stevens, and sees himself as distinctly apart from them in fundamental ways—perhaps, and at his best, more related to Robert Frost and William Carlos Williams. Also, the book offers one of the first and best characterizations of Frieda. Often ignored or considered crudely, Frieda through Bynner's eyes is a woman of great personality and sensitivity who played a central role in Lawrence's life and art.

Bynner brought out a collection of poems in 1955, *Book of Lyrics,* and then his final book, *New Poems 1960*. The first contained previously published lyrics and some new ones, often capturing moments of delicate reflection on the conditions of age and the fine, special pleasures it can bring. It is a confident book, as if Bynner had decided not to compete anymore with the poetic world that had passed him by. It is as if the poems reflect the acceptance of his age and reputation, very much in the spirit of the Laotzu.

A Stream

> Cool, moving, fruitful and alive I go,
> In my small run reflecting all the sky.
> I see through trees, I see through melting snow,
> I see through riffles which the wind and I
> Have made, and through the shadow of man,
> Nor know where I arrive, where I began.

Winter Morning

The hills for miles are stricken into one,
Whiter and simpler than oblivion,
Alive with sudden snow, with sudden sun.

The Wintry Mind

Winter uncovers distances, I find,
And so the blowing of the wintry mind
Takes leaves away, till there is left behind
A wide cold world. And so the heart grows blind
To the earth's green motions lying warm below
Field upon field, field upon field, of snow.

The second book is a late return with force to the spirit of the Spectra poems. It may have been inspired by an account of the Spectra poems written by William Jay Smith and published in 1961, *The Spectra Hoax*. Smith had read the Spectra poems to Bynner in 1958, and Bynner reported that "he went to bed each night with his head filled, as it were, with the specters of *Spectra*." Smith, in his introduction to *The Works of Witter Bynner: Light Verse and Satires*, continues the story of these late and eccentric poems: "He explained that while he slept complete poems came to him; on awakening he would put them down in a notebook just as he had received them." Smith believes that "some of the images seem far too polished to have risen untouched from the depths of dream." He compares favorably the *New Poems 1960* to aspects of the work of Theodore Roethke, John Berryman, and T. S. Eliot. The critic Douglas Day, in a 1961 review of the book, refers to the Eliot connection after quoting these two poems of Witter Bynner's:

When we read
Any other time would have done
    But not now
    Because now there is no time
And when there is no time
    It only stands still on its own center
    Waiting to be found

Once upon a time somebody will unwind it
    And then what a time
    In no time at all

or (one of the best poems in the volume)

> All tempest
> Has
> Like a navel
> A hole in its middle
> Through which a gull may fly
> In silence

we think of Eliot's still point of the turning world, timeless, quiet, and unchanging. There is in Bynner's poetry, as in *Ash Wednesday* and *Burnt Norton*, the sense that patience, humility, and introspection are the qualities that lead to the attainment of the still point. . . . The passages in Bynner's poems which evoke recollections of Eliot are, moreover, part of a theme which is seriously taken up several times in the book, and which seems indeed to be a product of the poet's subconscious: the necessary presence in life of silent recesses into which creatures can creep for quiet and solace from the confusions of the time-driven world.

Day further says: "It is possible that the strict rules of Chinese poetry become so natural to him that his dream-visions can come neatly packaged out of his subconscious as *shih* poems of the T'ang Dynasty."

New Poems is startlingly modern for a poet who was then and is now usually considered by critics as old-fashioned. Conceived in the moment just before waking, jotted onto a large pad with a thick pencil, in the dark, since he could no longer see well, the poems read like inquiries into the mysteries and absurdities of our long, strange lives. They offer no answers, but they open many vistas. They are poems such as Prospero might have written; they are the wise, odd words of an old man who is in touch still with some aspect of that special excitement one can find in life. They are a brilliant and original conclusion to an often brilliant, original life, written in a style very much Bynner's own. It is interesting what William Carlos Williams wrote about the book in a 1960 letter to the poet Winfield Townley Scott: "One of his best, he got hold of something and let himself go. The result was an unqualified piece of work that will be hard to equal for many a long day."

Williams saw something in these poems that is not easily seen. The poems can seem too light, or too abstract and disconnected as they reach in directions not easily understood. As with so much in Bynner's work, one wonders where to place them. They are at once obvious and difficult to penetrate. Here, for once, Bynner seems to be approaching aspects of Pound, Eliot, and Stevens, but very much in his own way, without pessimism or a conscious philosophy and with a persistence of humor and generosity. Late in 1960 Bynner wrote to a friend an explanation of one of the *New Poems;* it is a statement that effectively captures the serious, even profound quality under the seemingly light surface of the poems, as it also reveals his own state of mind, his gentle acceptance, as he approaches the end of his life.

> Crumbling from these were those
> And that was it
>
> No answer could have been so true
> And yet in the crowd around
> Not one believed
>
> For the answer was a man's
> Which we know well
> Would never do
> In weather so adroit

I wonder if my explanation which follows will not be as valid and natural to you as it is to me. The first stanza means the successive generations of death, and I did not write "Crumbling from those were these . . ." because I meant that there would be crumbling from these others like those—the successive generations of dead. The second stanza means simply, in spite of colossal evidence that human life disappears, no one really believes it as long as he himself exists. The third stanza means that, though each man disbelieves it about himself, he cannot resist evidence that the weather of time adroitly gradually blows the other man away. I trust that my explanation is not as difficult for you as the poem—even hope that it will make the poem ring clearly—that its concern is the evidence of individual immortality.

≡

The chronicle of the end had begun: first his majordomo in Chapala, Ysidoro Pulido, dies in 1956; his brother, Tim, dies after an operation in 1959; Rita Padilla dies in 1963, after three weeks in a coma. Then the great shock: Bob Hunt dies on January 18, 1964, of a heart attack as he is about to go to Chapala alone to bring back some of their possessions. Hunt says, "I feel a vertigo," and he is dead. There had been warnings— at least two serious heart attacks—that he refused to heed. He could face these attacks only in the most diverting way, as if their true seriousness were just too great to accept. He said of himself in a letter to a friend:

Then, add to troubles, I've been having a series of small "heart attacks" (not real coronaries, god wot; but a form of angina pectoris, or whatever they call it). I get pains in me chest and funny hot-wire feelings and weakness in me left arm and wrist; hard breathing, etc. etc. Now did you EVER!? What *next!* But I'm better now and munch on dynamite pills (nitroglycerin tablets) from time to time,— and take another green pill every 12 hours,—and feel *much* better. But I must cut down on me drinking, and not lift heavy things, etc, etc. Such a bore!

There is another side to this avoidance that is evident from the letter of instruction Hunt wrote the day before he died and gave to John Meigs, a friend from San Patricio, New Mexico, who was to take care of Bynner while Hunt was in Chapala. Hunt conveys his concern in humor, perhaps as a way of making that concern less painful and more palpable to himself.

January 17, 1965

MEMORANDA TO JOHN MEIGS (ALIAS REDBEARD):
THINGS TO DO AND NOT TO, PLEASE:
(MOST IMPORTANT!)

1. Dorothy is to be called any time for any sort of help. Her unlisted phone number is 3-8243. Bill will probably answer—but though a Frenchman, he is broadminded about Dorothy's men friends. Her street address is 609 Abeyta and mailing address: P.O. Box 528.

2. Mrs. Spurrier usually wakes Hal a few minutes before 12:00, but you might check from my bedroom on the inter-com (dialing 2 and be sure the inter-com button is down) to see that he is up. Sometimes he will dial you back to say if he wants his back fixed.

3. Have lunch every day if you can, you will be seeing enough of him at other times, but primarily to read his mail. Please see that business mail which goes to Dorothy is marked (especially anything from the Hanover Bank or bills to be paid) by Hal and see that they get to Dorothy; otherwise they are apt to get into Hal's personal mail and tucked into his pockets or lost. When the

door bell rings three times (at 1:15 p.m.) *rush* to the door and let Dorothy in. (!) (Three rings at 5:20 means Bill C.)

4. MOST IMPORTANT: Hal has promised me on the family Bible that he will go to bed each night around midnight—certainly not one minute after 12:30. I know you're not a night-hawk nor a late sleeper in the morning; but please if and when you can at night see that Hal gets upstairs and into bed and takes his pills before you yourself retire. It is this period between midnight and around four in the morning that we all worry about Hal. He often dozes with a lighted cigar in the library and when he gets up for whatever reason, his circulation is bad in his ankles and he can take a spill. Therefore once again. even if you have to use force as against your own personal charm, *beat* him and see that he is in bed before you retire. . . .

7. Hal and I agree that unless he has to go to a doctor, it's best not to take him out in this cold weather even for social drinks. Much better let friends come to him and you. If you have to drive Hal to doctors or wherever, please watch his hands in getting caught in the door and always take a flashlight to help him back after dark. . . .

16. Although Hal hates to admit this, he has great difficulty in locating his clothes, also knowing whether they match or are clean or not. Although he'll never ask you, I know he'll appreciate your helping him pick out what he is to wear when he dresses.

17. Order Imperial Whiskey and Ballantine's Ale also small soda water when needed from Washington Avenue liquor store, Telephone: 2-1081. Delivery boy's name is Nabor. They are open till 9:30, but if you order after dark please make sure both outside light switches are on to help the delivery man. . . .

20. If and when you take Hal out for doctors or drinks or whatever, it is best for Hal to use front door steps. He can use your arm or, what he likes is to have you be one step ahead of him. Under no circumstances let him use the steep steps by the kitchen. However, if he insists on using those stairs, especially upon returning, walk sort of behind him. He has a tendency to tilt backwards and fall and you'd be there to catch him. *Front steps are better*. He has key to front door. . . .

This has been freshly dictated by Robert Nichols Montague Hunt who wishes to take this opportunity to thank you once again for your patience in reading this and your helpfulness in general.

Perhaps what is here—the deep concern and love, unexpected in someone whose habits were so extreme, and the attention to detail, but in such an open, easy, fresh, and unpained way—make one understand how Bynner could say at the end of a letter written the day Hunt died: "In spite of appearances at times, Bob was the kindest and truest fellow I ever met and I suppose it was easier for him to go this way instead of to drag through illness. But living without Bob is as you know almost unintelligible to yours faithfully, Hal."

Their love is clearly evident in these documents, but it seems there is so much more feeling expressed in Hunt's instructions than in Bynner's pained but careful epitaph for his lover. Hunt gave, if anything, always too much, and Bynner was never certain how far to go to share in intimacy, to risk commitment that might endanger him. John Meigs, the man who was with Bynner when Hunt died and who remained with Bynner for the next six months, said Bynner never once mentioned Hunt's death, except to confirm that Hunt's ashes were buried in the garden of his house on Atalaya Hill.

The confusion after Hunt's death is endless. Hunt had not put his legal affairs in order. After Miegs leaves, there is no one to stay in the house with Bynner, and now he cannot be left alone: he cannot see or always keep his balance, and he is prone to fall over the edge of a carpet or on the stairs. Bynner is not able to cope with all there is to do, nor is his secretary. Bob's own house, the one he had so carefully worked on, is willed to Bynner, who gives it to St. John's College, but what about Hunt's furniture and books? Bynner answers letters but forgets a few weeks later whether he has already written, nor can a carbon be found; yet the letter has been answered. Much of the fine Indian silver has been given to local museums, and the Chinese scrolls and jade to the Roswell Museum in Roswell, New Mexico, but there is so much more to decide on. What else should he do; what is right to do? Then there is a heart attack in the fall of 1964—but an unusually good recovery.

Almost one year exactly from the date of Hunt's death, on January 16, 1965, clearly conscious of that event, Bynner had a severe stroke. He never recovered, never again gained full control of his mind. Nursed much as a child, dressed, fed, and bathed, often silent or speaking nonsense, seldom able to recognize anyone but expressing fears of being left alone, cared for by round-the-clock nurses, he persisted in staying alive until June 1, 1968, when he went quickly from sleep into death, without any movement at all. His ashes were buried with Hunt's in the garden of the house on Atalaya Hill. A carved stone image of a weeping dog, bought by them in Mexico, was placed on the grave.

All his life Bynner had fought his fear of being alone and had created around himself a devoted audience to whom he had been extraordinarily generous. He had constructed his life so that he would not succumb to the fear of isolation, as had his father and grandfather, his mother, and so many others in his family who had gone mad or who had tried to escape in drink or in illness. He had tried to mold a life that was amusing, bright, clear, and simple, with few disarming or troublesome personal contacts, few intimacies that might force him to examine relations too closely. At the end he feared that "his family," as he called the nurses, might leave him. He would ask if the family loved one another; he wanted to be certain they did, for without love he feared they would not stay.

In "Epithalamium and Elegy," a poem he wrote in 1925, he said: "My single constancy is love of life," and in the poem it is life he has married in an open, unconditional union. Alone, as Bynner believed man is, he marries not another human being, for human union is too dangerous to sanity, too transitory. Yet in marrying life, one embraces death. There is, then, no other way, but one accepts this inevitable condition. It is, for Bynner, the reality of life.

> My single constancy is love of life:
> Because we have entered no such formal pact
> As dulls devotion between man and wife,
> No bland acknowledgment, no binding fact,
> No mingling of betrothal with divorce,
> No dated bliss, no midnight certitude,
> No sad necessity, no matter of course,
> No pallid answer saying why we wooed;
> Because she lets me love her as I can
> Moment by moment, moments that always come
> Beyond the calculation of a man
> For joy or pain, for epithalamium
> Or for elegy, and because, when I am spent,
> Life shall have had her way, shall be content
> Still to confer the sweet bewilderment
> On someone else, shall loosen her lovely hair
> To the wind, shall turn with bountiful intent
> Toward anyone at all, and I not there,

Shall offer cool papayas, pale bamboo
And amorous guava to a later comer,
And none of her gifts, not even a drop of dew,
To me who had received them many a summer.
These are not harlotries but only joy,
These are the very tiptoes of delight.
This is the happiness she gives a boy
With nothing of wickedness, nothing of spite
In that immense, delicious, naked bed
Where anyone may lie, except the dead . . .
But I shall leave her. All that there is of rest
Shall be little enough, after so much of love.
Wherever I move, she is there. Her open breast
Offers the tenderness I am dying of.
Her arm along my body like a snake
Has softly wound me into rings of sleep
And, every time again, stings me awake
And drowns me in her rhythms deep and deep . . .
Can I be tragical, in having had
My love of life by herself subdued?
Since I am satiate with joy, can I be sad
In leaving? All that there is of solitude
Shall be little enough, after this vast embrace.
Give her some younger lover in my place.

≡≡≡

Bynner's will left a substantial sum of money to establish the Witter Bynner Foundation for Poetry, which is operated from Santa Fe and funds programs throughout the country that support the work of poets. His name is generally known for this unusual and admirable activity. A five-volume edition of Bynner's selected poems, light verse, translations, prose, and letters was supported by the foundation and published in the late seventies and early eighties. The selected poems and selected letters are still available in hardcover and the Chinese translations are in paperback. As a separate edition, *The Way of Life according to Laotzu* is in print and is the most likely book anyone today would know. Oddly, a reprint exists of the 1913 edition of his one-act play *Tiger*. And *Iphigenia in Tauris* is in print in the University of Chicago edition of the complete Greek plays, edited by David Grene and Richard Lattimore.

Bynner's house was willed to St. John's College in Santa Fe and for many years was used as a dormitory for the students. Now it has been sold. For a time it was an inn that also presented small exhibitions of local artists. Some people want to make it a center for writers. Most people who have come to Santa Fe in the last twenty-five years do not know who Witter Bynner is, and most students of literature have never read a poem of his because Bynner's work seldom appears in any anthology.

Bibliography

Works by Witter Bynner

Against the Cold. New York: Alfred A. Knopf, 1940.

The Beloved Stranger: Two Books of Song & a Divertisement for the Unknown Lover. New York: Alfred A. Knopf, 1919.

A Book of Love, translated from the French of Charles Vildrac. New York: E. P. Dutton & Company, 1923.

Book of Lyrics. New York: Alfred A. Knopf, 1955.

A Book of Plays. New York: Alfred A. Knopf, 1922.

Cake: An Indulgence. New York: Alfred A. Knopf, 1926.

A Canticle of Pan and Other Poems. New York: Alfred A. Knopf, 1920.

A Canticle of Praise. San Francisco: John Henry Nash, 1918

Caravan. New York: Alfred A. Knopf, 1925.

Eden Tree. New York: Alfred A. Knopf, 1931. Revised and reprinted in *Selected Poems* (1936).

Grenstone Poems: A Sequence. New York: Frederick A. Stokes Company, 1917. Revised and reprinted, New York: Alfred A. Knopf, 1926.

Guest Book. New York: Alfred A. Knopf, 1935.

Indian Earth. New York: Alfred A. Knopf, 1930.

Iphigenia in Tauris, translated from the Greek of Euripides. New York: Mitchell Kennerley, 1915. Reprinted in *A Book of Plays* (1922). Revised and reprinted in *The Complete Greek Tragedies: Euripides II,* edited by David Grene and Richard Lattimore. Chicago: University of Chicago Press, 1956.

The Jade Mountain, A Chinese Anthology: Being Three Hundred Poems of the T'ang Dynasty, 618–906, translated from the Chinese with Kiang Kang-hu. New York: Alfred A. Knopf, 1929. Revised and reprinted, 1939.

Journey with Genius: Recollections and Reflections concerning the D. H. Lawrences. New York: The John Day Company, 1951.

The Little King. New York: Mitchell Kennerley, 1914. Reprinted in *A Book of Plays* (1922).

The New World. New York: Mitchell Kennerley, 1915. Revised and reprinted, New York: Alfred A. Knopf, 1922.

New Poems 1960. New York: Alfred A. Knopf, 1960.

An Ode to Harvard and Other Poems. Boston: Small, Maynard & Company, 1907. Revised and reprinted in *Young Harvard: First Poems of Witter Bynner.* New York: Alfred A. Knopf, 1925.

The Persistence of Poetry. San Francisco: Book Club of California, 1929.

Pins for Wings, by Emanuel Morgan. New York: The Sunwise Turn, 1920.

Selected Poems, edited by Robert Hunt, with a critical preface by Paul Horgan. New York: Alfred A. Knopf, 1936.

The Sonnets of Frederick Goddard Tuckerman. New York: Alfred A. Knopf, 1931.

Spectra: A Book of Poetic Experiments, published with Arthur Davison Ficke under the names of Emanuel Morgan and Anne Knish. New York: Mitchell Kennerley, 1916.

The Spectra Hoax, by William Jay Smith. Middletown, Connecticut: Wesleyan University Press, 1961.

Take Away the Darkness. New York: Alfred A. Knopf, 1947.

Tiger. New York: Mitchell Kennerley, 1913. Reprinted in *A Book of Plays* (1922).

The Way of Life according to Laotzu: An American Version. New York: The John Day Company, 1944.

The Works of Witter Bynner: Selected Poems; Light Verse and Satires; The Chinese Translations; Prose Pieces; Selected Letters. General editor James Kraft. New York: Farrar Straus Giroux, 1978–81.

Critical Works on Witter Bynner

The papers of Witter Bynner were given at his death to the Houghton Library at Harvard University. This extensive collection contains letters to him and copies of letters he wrote, journals, notebooks, clippings, and photographs. The research for this volume is based largely upon this material, especially the letters, of which at the Houghton Library and elsewhere there are more than seven thousand.

The principal sources for other Bynner material are the Beinecke Rare Book and Manuscript Library at Yale University; the Harry Ransom Humanities Research Center, University of Texas at Austin; the Haniel Long Papers in the Department of Special Collections, Research Library, University of California at Los Angeles; and the Bancroft Library, University of California at Berkeley.

For a complete history of Bynner's works and articles on him, see the bibliography by Robert O. Lindsay listed below. Since the publication of this bibliography, there has been little written about Bynner. The book *The Spectra Hoax* contains an extensive essay by William Jay Smith. Each of the volumes in *The Works of Witter Bynner* contains a critical essay: in *Selected Poems,* by Richard Wilbur and James Kraft; in *Light Verse and Satires,* by William Jay Smith; in *The Chinese Translations,* by Burton Watson and David Lattimore; and in *Prose Pieces* and *Selected Letters*, by James Kraft.

The companion volume to *Who Is Witter Bynner?* is the anthology *The Selected Witter Bynner*, edited by James Kraft and also published by the University of New Mexico Press. It contains a representative selection of Bynner's works.

The following is a selection of works on Bynner that reflect various aspects and different periods of his career. It should be noted that there is no single critical work on his career other than those just mentioned and almost no reference to him in current critical volumes.

Austin, Mary. "Soil of New Mexico." *New York Herald: Books,* September 8, 1929, pp. 5–6.

Benét, William Rose. "The Phoenix Nest: Contemporary Poetry." *Saturday Review of Literature,* June 1, 1935, pp. 18–19.

——. "The Phoenix Nest: Contemporary Poetry." *Saturday Review of Literature,* December 5, 1936, p. 40.

Blackmur, Richard P. "Versions of Solitude." *Poetry,* January 1932, pp. 217–21.

Boorman, Howard L. *Biographical Dictionary of Republican China, Volume I.* New York: Columbia University Press, 1967. See "Chiang K'ang-hu" (or, as WB wrote, "Kiang Kang-hu"), pp. 338–44.

Chauvenet, Dorothy M. "Secretary to Witter Bynner." *Santa Fean,* November 1981, pp. 8–9.

Colony, Horatio. "Witter Bynner—Poet of Today." *Literary Review,* Spring 1960, pp. 339–61.

Day, Douglas. "The New Old Poetry of Witter Bynner." *Shenandoah,* Winter 1961, pp. 3–11.

Deutsch, Babette. "Bitterness and Beauty." *New Republic,* February 10, 1926, pp. 338–39.

——. "Two Solitudes." *The Dial,* October 4, 1919, pp. 301–302.

Ficke, Arthur Davison "The Luminous Chinese Sage." *Poetry,* April 1945, pp. 40–42.

Fitts, Dudley. "Mr. Bynner's Nimble Versification." *New York Times Book Review,* June 15, 1947, p. 4.

——. "Poetry and Tradition." *Saturday Review of Literature,* October 26, 1940, p. 16.

Flanner, Hildegarde. "Witter Bynner's Poetry." *University of Kansas City Review,* June 1940, pp. 269–74.

Francke, Kuno. *Young Harvard: First Poems of Witter Bynner.* Foreword by Dr. Kuno Francke. New York: Alfred A. Knopf, 1925.

Haber, Tom Burns, ed. *Thirty Housman Letters to Witter Bynner.* New York: Alfred A. Knopf, 1957.

Horgan, Paul. "Details on Greatness." *Saturday Review of Literature,* August 18, 1951, pp. 9–10.

——. "In the Autumn of a Poet's Life a Second Flowering." *New York Times Book Review,* October 16, 1960, p. 20.

———. *Selected Poems,* by Witter Bynner. Critical preface by Paul Horgan. New York: Alfred A. Knopf, 1936.

Jarrell, Randall. "Poets: Old, New and Aging." *New Republic,* December 9, 1940, pp. 797–800.

Lindsay, Robert O. *Witter Bynner: A Bibliography.* Albuquerque: University of New Mexico Press, 1967.

Long, Haniel. "Mr. Bynner's Philosophy of Love." *Poetry,* February 1920, pp. 281–83.

Masters, Edgar Lee. *Grenstone Poems: A Sequence,* by Witter Bynner. Introductory note by Edgar Lee Masters. New York: Alfred A. Knopf, 1926.

Monroe, Harriet. "The Little King." *Poetry,* May 1915, p. 97.

———. "Mr. Bynner in the South-West." *Poetry,* August 1930, pp. 276–78.

———. "New Books of Verse." *Poetry,* December 1915, pp. 147–48.

Pearce, T. M. "Guest Book." *New Mexico Quarterly,* August 1935, pp. 211–12.

———. "Selected Books." *New Mexico Quarterly,* February 1937, pp. 68–70.

Reedy, William Marion. *The Beloved Stranger,* by Witter Bynner. Preface by William Marion Reedy. New York: Alfred A. Knopf, 1930.

Rodman, Selden. "Classic and Modern." *New York Times Book Review,* January 1, 1956, p. 4.

Rudnick, Lois Palken. *Mabel Dodge Luhan: New Woman, New Worlds.* Albuquerque: University of New Mexico Press, 1984. See chapter 7 on Luhan and Bynner.

Schorer, Mark. " 'People Dislike Me.' " *New York Times Book Review,* July 29, 1951, pp. 3, 18.

Scott, Winfield Townley. "Nothing is Static." *The Nation,* November 5, 1960, pp. 352–53.

Slack, Claudia. "A Centennial Party for Witter Who?" *Santa Fe Reporter,* August 20, 1981, pp. 23–24, 26.

Smith, William Jay. "Witter Bynner." In *The Penguin Companion to American Literature,* edited by Malcolm Bradbury, Eric Mottram, and Jean Franco. New York: McGraw-Hill, 1971.

Stanford, Donald E. "The Best of Bynner." *Hudson Review,* Summer 1983, pp. 389–98.

Tate, Allen. "Verse." *The Nation,* December 1925, p. 680.

Tietjens, Eunice. "From the Chinese." *Poetry,* February 1930, pp. 289–92.

Udall, Sharyn R. *Spud Johnson and "Laughing Horse."* Albuquerque: University of New Mexico Press, 1994.

Untermeyer, Louis. "A Christmas Inventory." *The Bookman,* December 1925, pp. 495–96.

———. "Frustrated Adam." *Saturday Review of Literature,* October 10, 1931, p. 186.

Van Doren, Mark. "Books: Anglo-Saxon Adventures in Verse." *The Nation,* June 26, 1920, pp. 855a–57a.

Index

Bynner, Witter (*continued*)
111; and Annie Louise Bynner,
3–6, 88–89; and Willa Cather,
16; character, 2–3, 9–10, 13, 21–
23, 41, 90, 95, 104, 111; Chinese
influences on, 45, 98; community involvement in Santa Fe, 58;
companions, 17; controversy as professor, 49; and Charles Townsend
Copeland, 11; in Cornish, 23–24;
creative life, 36; daily routine in
Santa Fe, 58; death, 111; democracy and, 7, 24, 36; described by
Jessie Rittenhouse, 21; description
of relationship with Hunt, 100–
101; diary, 21–22; diary entries
for 6 October–18 November 1902,
16; diary entry for 8–9 April 1904,
19; diary entry for 14–15 April
1904, 20; diary entry from 1911,
24; eulogy for Paul Thévenaz, 47–
48; explanation of *New Poems,* 107;
family, 4, 22–23, 90; family responsibilities, 12–13; fascination
with atom bomb, 98; final years,
2, 107, 110; finances, 85; foreign
culture and, 15–16; Greek drama
and, 2; habits, 11; as "Hal," 12;
at Harvard, 8–13; and O. Henry,
16; and Hispanic Americans, 2;
homosexuality, 23–24, 62, 84–85,
90–93; illnesses, 21–22, 50–51,
61, 98–99, 101, 110; lack of recognition, 86, 101; later years, 95, 98,
102; lectures, 38–49; lecture tour
(1922), 49–51; letter from Caroline
Naomi Bynner, 36; letter from Rita
Padilla, 59; letter to Albert Bender,
63; letter to Annie Louise Bynner
(1932), 85; letter to Arthur Ficke,
63; letter to Robert Hunt, 84, 97;
literary awards, 12; loss of popu-
larity, 61–62; marriage and, 41; at
McClure's, 14, 16; as Emanuel Morgan, 2, 39, 60; mother's influence

on, 6; photograph of grave site, *83;*
photograph of home in Chapala,
78; photograph of home on Buena
Vista (1977), *83;* photograph of
Santa Fe home, *76;* photograph of
study in Cornish, *29;* play writing,
36; poetry, 9, 11, 16, 42–44, 60;
possessions, 49–50, 110; provisions
of will, 112–13; quoted, 1–4, 7–
10, 12, 14–15, 18–19, 21, 23–24,
37–38, 48, 51, 61–63, 84, 88–90,
95, 98–103, 105–7, 110–12; relationship with Annie Louise Bynner,
88–89; relationship with Caroline Naomi Bynner, 8; relationship
with Jeanie Ernst, 8; relationship
with Arthur Ficke, 41–42; relationship with Robert Frost, 86–87;
relationship with Robert Hunt,
63–64, 84, 100, 110; relationship
with Henry James, 17; relationship
with Kiang Kang-hu, 44–45; relationship with Lawrences, 52–55;
relationship with Haniel Long, 93–
95; relationship with Mabel Dodge
Luhan, 52–58; relationship with
Edna St. Vincent Millay, 2, 41–42;
relationship with Rita Padilla, 59;
relationship with Ezra Pound,
1–2; relationship with Lynn Riggs,
50; relationship with Wallace
Stevens, 19–21; relationship with
Paul Thévenaz, 42, 47–48; relationship with William Butler Yeats,
18; in Santa Fe, 2, 59; seventieth-
birthday message, quoted, 103;
social awareness and, 37; social life,
17, 22, 49, 58–59; study of language, 9; and suffrage movement,
12, 24; support of Franklin D.
Roosevelt, 2; teaching career, 49;
travels, 2, 6, 14–16, 42, 45, 50, 53,
58, 99, 101–2; views on life, 91;
World War I and, 42; World War II
and, 42, 96; writing and, 23, 36, 62

Bynner, Witter, images of: by Ansel Adams (1951), *81;* at age seventeen, *27;* at age seventy-five (1956), *81;* at age three, *25;* with Edwin and Annie Louise Bynner, *26;* with Patricio Calabaza and Rafael Lovato (1922), *65;* on camel, *35;* with Arthur Ficke, *32;* with great Buddha in Japan, *33;* at Greek Theater, Berkeley, *31;* with Ho Chi in Peking, *34;* with Kiang Kang-hu, *31;* with D. H. and Frieda Lawrence (1922), *67;* with Frieda Lawrence and Willard Johnson (1922), *68;* by Margreth Mather (1928), *71;* in 1918, *32;* painted with Clifford McCarthy and Louisa Pugh by Russell Cheney (1929), 71; portrait by Arnold Genthe, *30;* portrait by Henriette Wyeth Hurd (1939), *76;* publicity photograph, *30;* with Ysidoro Pulido, *79;* with Ysidoro Pulido and family, *79;* with Carlota St. Gaudens, *28;* with Charles Stigall, *80;* after stroke (1965), *82;* by Carl Van Vechten (1933), *77;* as youth, *25–27*

Bynner, Witter, works of: *Against the Cold,* 90; *Anygirl,* 36; "At the Last," 42–43; "Beautiful Mexican," 61; *Beloved Stranger, The,* 42, 46–47, 60; *Book of Love, A,* 60; *Book of Lyrics,* 104; *Book of Plays, A,* 60; *Cake,* 55–57, 60; *Canticle of Pan,* 60; *Caravan,* 48, 60; "Chinese People in Poetry," 96; "Countryman, A," 61; "Dead in the Philippines," 99; "Defeat," 7–8; "D. H. Lawrence," 53; "Driftwood," 43; "Drinking Alone with the Moon," 45–46; *Eden Tree,* 62, 84, 90–92; "Episode of Decay," 92, 95; "Epithalamium and Elegy," 60, 111; "Farewell to a Friend, A," 46; "Foreigner, A," 53; "George

Meredith's Style," 12; *Grenstone Poems,* 42; *Guestbook,* 86; "Heart of China, The," 51; *Indian Earth,* 53, 60, 88; *Jade Mountain, The,* 1, 60; *Journey with Genius: Recollections and Reflections concerning the D. H. Lawrences,* 1, 53–54, 104; *Kit,* 36; "Lightning," 47; "Lorenzo," 53–55; *Mechanic, The,* 36; *New Poems 1960,* 104–7; *New World,* 36–38; *Ode to Harvard, An,* 9, 12, 62; *Ode to Harvard and Other Poems, An,* 19, 36; "Opus 6," 40; "Opus 40," 39–40; *Persistence of Poetry,* 60–61; *Pins for Wings,* 60; Pueblo Indian poems, 60; "Revolution," 10–11; "Robert Frost," 87; *Selected Poems,* 86; *Spectra* poems, 2, 86, 105; "Spring and a Mother Dead," 90; "Stream, A," 104; *Take Away the Darkness,* 7, 99; *Tiger,* 36, 112; "To My Mother concerning a Chapala Sunset," 88; translation of Euripides' *Iphigenia in Tauris,* 2, 36, 112; translation of T'ang poems, 44; "Two Windows," 99–100; "Wall, The," 47; *Way of Life according to Laotzu,* 1, 97, 104, 112; "Winter Morning," 104; "Wintry Mind, The," 105; "Word or Two with Henry James, A," 17; *Young Harvard,* 9; "Young Visit with George Meredith, A," 15

Bynner family, 8

C

Cabeza de Vaca, Alvar Nuñez, 93

Cake (Bynner), 55–57, 60, 63

Calabazo, Patricio, photographed with Bynner and Rafael Lovato (1922), *65*

Canticle of Pan (Bynner), 60

Caravan (Bynner), 48, 60

Cather, Willa, 16

Century (Gilder), 17

Chapala: poems on, 60–61; social life of, 97

Chauvenet, Dorothy, 98

"Chinese People and Poetry" (Bynner), 96

communism, 2

conscientious objectors, 49

Copeland, Charles Townsend, 11

Corbin, Alice. *See* Henderson, Alice Corbin

"Countryman, A" (Bynner), 61

Courant, Edwin Tyler Bynner as editor, 4

Croly, Herbert; as editor of *New Republic,* 23; *Promise of American Life, The,* 23

Cullen, Countee, 7

D

Day, Douglas, quoted, 106

"Dead in the Philippines" (Bynner), 99

"Defeat" (Bynner), 7–8

DeMille, Cecil B., 36

Dewey, John, 24

"D. H. Lawrence" (Bynner), 53

"Driftwood" (Bynner), 43

"Drinking Alone with the Moon" (Bynner), 45–46

Duncan, Isadora, 2, 36, 112

E

Eden Tree (Bynner), 62, 84, 90–92

Eisenstein, Sergei, 85

Eliot, T. S., 57; *Sweeney Agonistes,* 57, 60

"Episode of Decay" (Bynner), 92, 95

"Epithalamium and Elegy" (Bynner), 60, 111

Ernst, Jeanie, quoted, 4, 8

Euripides, *Iphigenia in Tauris,* 2, 36, 112

Evans, John, 53

Everyman, 36

F

"Farewell to a Friend, A" (Bynner), 46

Fehling, Hans, 99

Ficke, Arthur, 2, 12, 38; death, 98; as Anne Knish, 2, 39; marriage and, 41; "Opus 118," 39; photographed with Gladys Ficke and Robert Hunt in Chapala (1935), *73;* quoted, 10; relationship with Bynner, 41–42; relationship with Edna St. Vincent Millay, 41–42; writing career, 41

Fiske, Minnie Maddern, 12

"Foreigner, A" (Bynner), 53

France, described by Bynner, 14

Frost, Robert, 86–87

G

"George Meredith's Style" (Bynner), 12

Germany, described by Bynner, 14–15

Gilder, Richard Watson, as editor of *Century,* 17

Grenstone Poems (Bynner), 42

Guestbook (Bynner), 86

H

Harland, Henry, as editor of *Yellow Book,* 17

Harris, Henriette, 98, 101; quoted, 89

"Heart of China, The" (Bynner), 51

Henderson, Alice Corbin, 50–52

Henderson, William Penhallow, 53

Henry, O. *See* Porter, William Sydney

History of the Origin of the Town of Clinton, Massachusetts, 1653–1865, 4

Hollywood Reporter (Kennedy), 99

Horgan, Paul, 63; introduction to *Selected Poems,* 86; letter from Robert Hunt, 85–86

Housman, A. E., 1, 15

Hughes, Langston, 7

Hunt, Robert, 2; as architect, 64; bitterness of, 100; character, 63–64; death, 107–11; described by